Foreword

Our 'My Favourite Person 2009' poetry competition
attracted young aspiring poets to show their
admiration for those who have made an impact in
their life. What better way to let those closest know
how much they are appreciated.

We are delighted to present this thoughtful
collection. After reading through the hundreds of
entries it is clear the amount of enthusiasm and
love that went into writing these poems, therefore
we hope you'll agree they are an inspiring and
heart-warming read.

Young Writers was established in 1991 to promote
poetry and creative writing to schoolchildren and
encourage them to read, write and enjoy it. Here
at Young Writers we are sure you'll agree that this
special edition achieves our aim and celebrates
today's wealth of young writing talent. We hope you
enjoy this anthology for many years to come.

My Favourite Person

Inspired By You

Edited by Donna Samworth

First published in Great Britain in 2010 by:

 Young **Writers**

Young Writers
Remus House
Coltsfoot Drive
Peterborough
PE2 9JX
Telephone: 01733 890066
Website: www.youngwriters.co.uk

Contents

The Poems

My Favourite People

My mum

She helps me through tough times in my life,
She mends me and my feelings,
She shows me the bright pathways ahead
And she even helps me in bed,
Here she comes,
The world's number one mum!

My dad

He takes me to all the fun games,
He helps me through my schoolwork
And just by magic, he defeats all my worries,
Nothing's scary when my dad's around,
Here he comes,
The world's number one dad!

My two brothers

Sometimes they can be nuisances,
But also like best friends,
I like having brothers,
Because they keep me company
And help me through things,
They are always the ones who stick up for me,
So, here they come,
The world's best brothers!

My best friend

My best friend never stops giving up,
She is really friendly and is there for me all the time,
We buy presents on every occasion,
My best friend is like a sister to me,
Here they come . . .

The world's number one's family and friends!

I thank you, God, for giving me perfect family and friends.

Charlotte Amy Lumb (10)

1

My Grandad

(Dedicated to my grandad - Norman Phillips, 1943-2007)

Thump, thump,
Thump, thump,
The heartbeat,
His heartbeat,
It doesn't last forever!

It wasn't long enough,
It never is,
Not when it's someone you really love,
I loved him!
Anyone who knew him loved him!

He was the best!

I didn't have enough time to really get to know him,
He was gone before I knew it,
I miss him,
His hands were so big and so strong,
Yet the softest and most gentle ever!

If you knew him,
If only you knew him,
He would amaze you!
He seemed to give out this warm feeling!
This warm, loving feeling!

He was the best!

So clever!
So kind!
So funny!

He could fix anything,
His farm is fantastic,
His wife *is* amazing!
He was so sweet, so nice,
I loved him and he loved me!

He would move his big, round glasses,
Up and down,
From behind his ears he would push them,
Up and down,

It would amaze me for hours!
It took me years to figure out how he did it!

So, there's my grandad,
In a nutshell,
The laughs,
The cries
And the sheer amazement of him!

He was the best!

Daniel Norman Cranstone (12)

My Sister, Danielle

My sister, Danielle, knows how to yell
And everywhere she goes, she casts her spell
I love her to bits
Even when she throws some fits
She has got long brown hair
And eyes that flash and stare
She loves her clothes and shoes
And has often been in the news

She loves to go out with her friends
And keep up with all the trends
Some nights she works in a restaurant
Whose reputation is excellent
She comes home late
And clashes the gate
Or, if she stays in for the night
We are likely to have a fight

She won a place at university
Which suited her personality
But when the day came when she had to go
I sobbed and cried and couldn't let go
We drove right down there in our car
I just hadn't realised it was quite so far
'Oh, sister, oh, sister, please don't go
Come home soon and say hello.'

Helena Johnsen (9)

I Love My Mum And Dad

I love you Mum and Dad, more than I can say!
I love you Mum more than I can say,
I'll love you tomorrow and I'll love you today.
I'll love you forever and ever and ever,
It's like our heart beat, beats together.
You have watched me grow for many years,
Through the ups and downs and the smiles and tears.
I'll never be ready to say goodbye,
Because if I did I would cry and cry.
My favourite thing in life is you,
And without you, I don't know what I would do.
You're clever, creative, helpful and fun,
I just want to say, 'You're the best mum!'
I love you Mum more than I can say,
I'll love you tomorrow and I'll love you today.
I just can't forget to thank my dad even when I'm naughty, unwell or sad.
So there's a few things I thank him for,
And I'll still thank him once I've walked through our door!
My dad's there when I'm feeling down!
My dad's there to get rid of my frown!
My dad's there to make me happy!
He was even there to change my nappy!
My dad's there to get me out of bed!
My dad's there when I've banged my head!
My dad's there to be very funny!
He is certainly there to spend some money!
My dad's there forever and ever!
My dad's there because we're always together!
My dad's been there since I was small!
He is definitely there watching me grow tall!
I thank you Dad for all these things,
And helping me with what the future brings!
Love from
Asha x

Asha Astbury (12)

4

Cloud

He is the mist
Forever moving
Consuming the darkness
A white shape looming.

He is the tiger
Which stands so proud
Sly and cunning
Not making a sound.

He is the spider
Weaving its web
The fly is caught
Its life starts to ebb.

He is the knight
Noble and strong
With his shining sword
Doing no wrong.

He is the shadow
Strange and quick
Always evolving
The masterful trick

He is the hand
Reaching far down
Lifting the burdens
Erasing the frown.

He is the cloud
His shape always changing
His enemies cut down
Himself still remaining.

The only Cloud.

Daniel Ryan (13)

My Beloved Grandad

There are celebrities, there's my family and friends,
Friendly teachers, and also I have furry pets.
Some of them, I have never met before,
Others, every day I keep seeing more and more.
But if one of them I would have to choose,
My favourite person would be my grandad, who always keeps me amused.

He knows funny jokes that lift me when I'm down,
To him I can talk for hours, and of boredom he'll never frown.
We used to always hunt for mushrooms, and help each other in everything,
He treated me like a prince, I treated him like a king.
We made things from wood and always had fun,
Every day to pick me up from my house he would enthusiastically come,
And during these days of spending time together,
Our love kept getting bigger and bigger and it will not end, never.

But sadly now, from each other we live far away,
An unbelievably long journey, everyone would say,
So, every single day my grandad I call,
And we talk for hours, in which we find unbelievable joy.
We see each other two, sometimes three times a year,
And during that time, there is nothing we fear.
Then, when we meet again, after a long time,
You should see the joy on our faces, you would probably cry.
Then, when I leave, for ages we are sad,
Most likely, if that happened to others, they would go mad.

My grandad is someone I simply can't imagine life without,
And will always, beyond no end, love.
These are the reasons, to him, this poem I dedicate.
Someone who I admire, my best ever mate.
When I am writing this, in my eyes there are tears.
But I want everyone to know about this, especially my peers.

Norbert Sobolak (12)

The Perfect Best Friend

My very favourite person,
As you must agree,
Has to be my best friend,
Her name is Emily!

Not once has she interrupted me,
Nor told me, 'You are wrong,'
She's been with me for seven years,
We've been best buddies so long!

She's really fun, but sometimes cheeky,
We always stay awake at night,
The next day we are very sleepy,
But at least I had a good time.

She never lets down my dreams,
She never is a pest,
She never tells my secrets, like
Ew, look at my new vest!

Lots of activities we do together,
Swimming and gymnastics,
On a Thursday and a Friday,
It is really quite fantastic!

All the letters she writes to me,
Are signed BFF,
Hopefully our friendship will last
And will never get less!

Lots of laughs we've had together,
Lots of time we've spent together,
All the things we've done together,
That's why she is the perfect best friend!

Anna Morse (10)

Monty, Monty

Monty, Monty,
My dog, Monty,
Black, brown
And white.

He barks,
He slobbers,
He chases the cat
And plays with the hedgehogs he finds in the leaves.

Monty, Monty,
My dog, Monty,
Black, brown
And white.

He scratches the door,
He runs in the mud,
He digs big holes
And rolls in the dirt.

Monty, Monty,
My dog, Monty,
Black, brown
And white.

He likes to chew toys
And eats all his food,
Even though he's naughty,
I love him lots and lots.

Monty, Monty,
My dog, Monty,
Black, brown
And white!

Fern Bayliss (10)

Dill

Dill never understood reason,
He barely lived a life,
But everything he could do,
Seemed filled with happiness and light.
He was never very stupid,
But never very bright,
No one understood him,
Through his short-lived life.
Eating was his hobby,
Nothing he did more,
Sleeping he found next in line,
But he was never known to snore.
People talked about him freely,
He never seemed to care,
If there was a crowd around,
He would stand and stare.
Thrice he bit,
In times gone by,
It was not in his nature,
So I can only wonder why.
But I always loved him dearly,
Because he was so cute,
You could tell he was always happy,
Even though he was mute.
For me, he was very special,
For all his weaknesses and fault,
Because he lifted my spirits,
When I needed it most.
(He was also rather big -
Well, for a guinea pig.)

David Warren (13)

The Warrior's Call

There he stands
Tall and proud
A fighter's soul
A fighter's mind
A steely look upon his face
A burning fire in his heart
No need for steel
Nor for wood
For he has courage
And he has words
His players look
Upon his face
They look for truth
They look for hope
The offence shudders
In his wake
The quiet patter
Of his feet
Strikes more fear
In a players heart
Than a lion fighting
In the dark
A body swift
A body strong
A fury hot
A composure cool
And when he gets the victory
So precious in his mind
The crowd will rush around him
His body on the line.

Ronan Mannion (13)

Bob Marley

'Get up, stand up
Stand up for your rights.'
Bob Marley is the man
Who rose to dizzying heights.
Calm and relaxed
He took reggae to the max.
Preaching peace and love
Between his fellow blacks.
Music was his passion
He started his own fashion.
His music created
Massive reactions.
In his own country there was civil unrest
Each side fought to be the best.
For him, it was his test
To put the war to rest.
Bob Marley was the best
But he is now at rest
Forever he will lie
But his music will never die.
His music is played every day
From December to May.
His creative ways
Will blow your mind away.
When one listens to his music, they are mellow
One begins to see yellow.
They forget about the facts
And are happy and relaxed.
Chilling and kicking it back
You begin to slack.

Zach Colgan (13)

My Sister

My sister is the best
When she wins
She spins
We have a pet goldfish
With fins
My sister jumps in the pool
But I think she's a fool
When she jumps
Her head bumps
When she has her bag
She nags
While she watches telly
She sees her favourite artist, Kelly
When she sleeps
Her phone bleeps
When she reads
The dogs leap
When she plays
She goes in a daze
When she writes
Her head pipes
When she lights
Her hair tights
When she sits
She spits
When she uses gel
She gets well
When she talks
She walks.

Laila Hersi (9)

My Cousin

My favourite person is my cousin.
She's nice and kind.
She's one in a million.
She's loving and caring.
She even gives to charity.
She's ambitious and responsible.
Whenever she sets a goal she achieves it.
My cousin loves learning.
Expanding her knowledge.
She's the cleverest person I know.
She's keen and willing.
She hates fighting though.
She and me think alike.
That's why we are like sisters.
But in some ways we are totally different.
I like searching the web all the time.
While she likes learning.
I prefer loud and noisy.
She prefers it quiet.
We may like different things.
But we will always be like sisters.
My cousin is very special to me.
I tell her all my secrets.
Whenever I need help she's there.
She always knows what to do.
Like cheering me up, making me smile.
Like all sisters we have our ups and downs.
But when I really count on her she's there.
I am pretty sure me and her will be friends forever.

Mahima Ali Zain (10)

My Favourite Person

My mum is . . .
A loving and caring,
A gigantic tickle monster

        Kind of mum.

My mum is . . .
A take me to the cinema,
A gigantic tickle monster

        Kind of mum.

My mum is . . .
A snuggle up on the sofa,
A take me on holiday,
A gigantic tickle monster

        Kind of mum.

My mum is . . .
A play with me,
A make lovely dinners,
A light the fire on Christmas Eve,
A gigantic tickle monster

        Kind of mum.

My mum is . . .
A tuck me in bed,
A read me stories,
A lovely cake maker,
A gigantic tickle monster

        Kind of mum.

But what she does best is being my mum!

Bethany McConville (9)

Simon Cowell

Simon Cowell, oh, Simon Cowell
Funny as can be
Simon Cowell, oh, Simon Cowell
You're the only one for me!
Simon Cowell, oh, Simon Cowell
Not scared to give your opinion
Simon Cowell, oh, Simon Cowell
I would like to be your minion
Simon Cowell, oh, Simon Cowell
I'm afraid you're just too cool
Simon Cowell, oh, Simon Cowell
Big mansion with a swimming pool
Simon Cowell, oh, Simon Cowell
My hero day and night
Simon Cowell, oh, Simon Cowell
I'm not going without a fight!
Simon Cowell, oh, Simon Cowell
You're the person I adore
Simon Cowell, oh, Simon Cowell
X Factor, rubbish, give some more!
Simon Cowell, oh, Simon Cowell
Your words are bold and true
Simon Cowell, oh, Simon Cowell
You have the trend that's new
Simon Cowell, oh, Simon Cowell
I hope that we stay close
Simon Cowell, oh, Simon Cowell
You're the one I love the most!

Hannah Walls (12)

With And Without

As I age, so do they,
Collecting memories as we travel,
Like old photographs,
Collecting dust,

None of us leads,
None of us follows,
We are equals,

We are twins, triplets, brothers and sisters,
We are nothing without each other,
But an unstoppable army together:

My super-duper, fun-loving, action hero, wicked
Friends!
I couldn't choose a favourite,
Anymore than a mother could pick her favourite child,

But if I aged without their love,
If memories were better off forgotten,
Rather than reliving the horrors of the past,

If I'd tried to lead,
Or maybe follow,
But end up on my own,

If I'd see twins, triplets, brothers, sisters,
That would be when I realise I'd be nothing, if I had no one,
Because sometimes we take them for granted:

Our super-duper, fun-loving, action hero, wicked
Friends!

Huw Thomas (12)

My Favourite Person

Groove a tap, tap
With a vivacious clap, clap
Her brilliant personality
Obstinately screams quality
Guiding me is her best feature
Which makes her a miraculous teacher
She cushions me from every harm
So she appears to be my good luck charm

Groove a tap, tap
With a vivacious clap, clap
She is truthful to them all
And picks me up at my every fall
She teaches me impressive lessons
And understands all of my expressions
Her love for me is a joyful wealth
Which keeps up my smile and health
Her expensive teaching I'll keep as treasure
Forever and ever!

Groove a tap, tap
With a vivacious clap, clap
Sometimes her scolding may seem unreasonable
But the morals hidden in them are unimprovable
'Life is a bumpy path,' she says
'To cross it there are many ways'
So give it a groove, a tap, tap
With a vivacious clap, clap
For my mum!

Moksh Sharma (10)

My Mum

My mum brought me up from the start
Turned me into who I am.
I know, it's a fact!
That not many people can state.
The most scariest threat cannot make us part.

My mum would sacrifice her life
For me and many others.
I know, it's a fact!
That not many people can state.
A mountain cannot stretch enough to stop us.

My mum's world revolves around me.
Yet I am not a spoilt brat.
I know, it's a fact.
That not many people can state.
A terrifying threat cannot frighten us.

My mum knows me inside and out.
Amazing, I know, but true.
I know, it's a fact!
That not many people can state.
The biggest hurdle cannot make us stumble.

My mum is a special person,
Most children would say, I know.
Now this is a fact.
Coming from the depth of my heart.
My mum is the best mum and person on Earth.

Amber Joyce (11)

My Favourite Person

On our bikes we go
Whizzing round the park
Even in the snow
Never in the dark.

Sam Smith (9)

18

My Sister

My sister is sweeter than sugar
Eyes like chocolate buttons
Cheeks like soft, squidgy marshmallows
And a small button nose

My sister has a cheeky smile
And the energy of a whirlwind
She has the brain of Albert Einstein
And a creative mind like Monet

She has a warm, sweet heart
But an irritating part
She loves to tease and get me in trouble
But inside, she doesn't mean it

She can be demanding
Often gets what she wants
It can get quite annoying
And is always hungry

She does have dirty habits
Like picking her nose
Pulling toenails off her toes
And poking out her tongue

Yet small and vulnerable
I cherish her
I protect her
My sister, sweeter than sugar.

Joseph Meracap (11)

My Sister

My favourite person can be neat,
My favourite person can be sweet,
My favourite person can be my best friend,
My favourite person can be . . . *great!*
My favourite person is my . . . *sister!*

Tiarna Andre (9)

No-One

No-one can see my best friend
Although I know she's there
She stays with me all the time
I take her everywhere

At school, she gives me encouragement
She always cheers me on
Even when I feel upset
And things go badly wrong

I often take her to the park
And shopping with my friends
I take her to so many places
Our adventures never end

I do have other friends
But they are not as close
She is so true to me
She never, ever boasts

She's better than celebrities
Who makes themselves so thin
And all the sporty athletes
That nearly always win

She beats the lot of them
Because she always cares
She is my best friend
She is always there.

Esther Bancroft (11)

Jordan!

Jordan is beautiful and young,
She likes horse riding and having fun.
She's a glamour model
And a full-time mum,
I wish I could be someone.

Kaitlyn Sophie Caudwell (9)

Who Could It Be?

My favourite person,
Now who could that be?
Maybe someone famous,
Friends or family.

My favourite people,
I picked from the three,
They are very special,
Because they are family.

But which one,
Maybe Grandad or Granny?
Uncle or auntie?
Grandpa and Nanny?

Brother or sister?
Mum or Dad?
But I have to choose,
Which would make others sad.

I've chosen two,
From the above,
The ones who are most special
The ones who I mostly love.

Firstly, my mum,
She is really fun
And then there's my dad,
Who never makes me sad.

Lewis Butroid (10)

Mum

M ums are funny and kind
U nconditional love you give to us
M ums are always caring
S miling constantly through good times and bad.

Anya Devaney (8)

My Favourite Beauty

I have many favourite people,
My mum, dad, cat called Roly,
I have many favourite friends,
But my favourite is Little Beauty.

She's a cute, naughty, cheeky pony,
She's chestnut with a clean, white blaze,
Beauty likes eating Polos,
Each rider she does amaze.

Beauty may not be a person,
But she's my favourite creature in all,
I'll always love Beauty the pony,
Even if, from her, I many times fall.

You can't help loving Beauty,
With her big, wide, horsey grin,
If ever Little Beauty smiles at you,
What trouble you'll soon be in.

She has this habit of bucking
And tossing her riders up high,
I'm usually Beauty's victim,
From her back, I many times fly.

But no matter what Beauty does to me,
I'll always love her so,
Beauty's my favourite playmate,
I want the whole world to know!

Enya Ratcliffe (12)

My Dad

My dad is a daring, brave soldier
He's noble and royal
He will never recoil
And his strength is as much as a boulder.

James Cook (9)

Vlad The Impaler

Bats fly in the dead of night
Wolves howl far out on the moors
Rotting corpses are always a sight
Especially when hanging from half-open doors.

Such regality
For such a part of gore
Such frailty
For such a creature wanting more.

Dark and dark
Through and through
Clark and hark
The night sings out
What only creatures can do.

A shadow in the fading light
A smile of gleaming white
A figure
Drenched in red
A figure
Leaning over her bed.

A bite, a scream
A fright, a disturbed dream
Vlad's back in town, he's out for blood
He's out to regain his crown.

He's back in blood.

Gregory Radmore (13)

Nice, Gentle And Kind

Hayley, my sister, is nice, gentle and kind,
As nice as a summer's day,
As gentle as a falling petal,
As kind as a chirping robin.

Gemma Ryall (10)

Who's My Favourite Person?

My favourite person,
My mum or my dad,
I love both of them,
Even when my days are bad.

My mum makes me smile,
When I am sad,
As well as my mother,
There is my dad.

My dad is so sporty,
So funny and smart,
But above all the compliments,
He has a good heart.

They are both kind,
So caring, so sweet,
My two loving parents,
So lovely to meet!

When I am troubled,
What must I do?
I'll go to my parents,
Of course, but who?

I love my mum;
I love my dad;
So help me choose my favourite person
Before I go mad!

Meljude Fajardo (11)

Edward

Playful, imaginative, but unpredictable,
Bouncy, funny, but shy,
Exciting, friendly, yet very mischievous,
Adventurous, but so am I!

Ailie McWhinnie (11)

My Tremendous Brother

I have a little brother called James
He likes to play lots of games
James sometimes can be very strange
But that is always likely to change

He has Matthew as his best friend
He only lives round the bend
Together they are really weird
Always so slow to be ever geared

He's an indoor boy
With an electronic toy
He thinks I'm boring
Because I don't skid on the new flooring

He loves to make me laugh
Even in the bath
Laughing always together
We always say, 'Whatever!'

My brother is really cool
Because he can sit down on the bottom of the pool
We love to play in the dark
Being as happy as a lark

Well, that is James
With electronic games
My brother will be with me
No matter what we see.

Eleanor Coleman (10)

My Friends

My friends they greet me with a big, warm smile for me,
Indicating everything's alright
We chat together without a bit of bother
For my friends and I are . . . *friends!*

Jacob Paul van Buren (10)

Jesus Means A Lot To Me

Jesus means a lot to me
That means a lot to me
I lift Him on high
So everyone can hear
He was born to be king
That means a lot to me

He made my wish come true
That means a lot to me
He made the Earth
He created life
He made me and my brother and Mum
I am so grateful for that

He died for us
To save our sins
I lift Him on high
So everyone can hear
He is king of all kings
I gratefully adore Him

Mary watched as You grew
Why did it have to be done
When You knew that her feelings of love were so strong?
I felt like Mary, Your mum
When I heard how You died

Always, He's my Saviour.

Alice Shannon Roberts (11)

My Mum

With jet-black hair and shiny teeth,
My mum is a very big treat,
She does the cooking and she makes everything so neat,
Mum, Mum, you're an enormous treat!

Kimani Turner (9)

Untitled

My mum is caring, sometimes a pain,
But loving her is always the same.
I've always had two sisters at home,
Which is cool, because I'm never alone.
But no more sister talk in this poem,
Because I'm gonna write something worth showing.
Listen carefully, listen well,
Because something is ready to tell.

My mum looks after me here and there,
Always ready with things to share.
Going on picnics, bike rides and more,
She's the best, that's for sure.
Cooking us food for us to survive,
She never gives up, always tries.
Getting us our uniform for our new school,
I just really think my mum is cool.
She's always gotten us anything we've wanted,
Sometimes stressed, but that never stops it.
Whatever it is, she's always there,
Her rules are good, always fair.

I'm sorry to end this, but there's too much to tell,
It could fill up this page,
But you know . . . well . . .

That I just really love my mum!

Poppy Tierney-Jones (11)

Baby Rhianna Best

She's small, she's cute, she's got a good cry,
Her feet are such an immaculate size,
When she's older she will rise,
And then end up telling lies,
As for now she's staying small,
Until she grows so, so tall.

Elisha Best (11)

My Favourite Godmother, Laura

Long, blonde hair, a lovely, beautiful face
She has a cute laugh
She's the perfect godmother.

My favourite godmother, Laura
Very kind and loving
She sends me lots of postcards
When she goes to another country.

My favourite godmother, Laura
She gives me lots of presents at Christmas
When she comes down
She always plays with me.

My favourite godmother, Laura
Just became a proper teacher
I'd love to be in her class
But she lives too far away.

My favourite godmother, Laura
Just got back from America
She sent me a postcard
Of the Statue of Liberty.

My favourite godmother, Laura
I think she is the best
Because she's kind, loving, caring
And I think the world of her!

Kyra Rogers (8)

The Greatest Teacher

She is the greatest teacher ever made
She excites pupils about English and DT
She listens to your dilemmas and helps you out
She has a strange sense of fashion but
She is great
She is the best.

Zoë Crouch (10)

My Favourite Person

My favourite person is Aanya
She loves watching the film Narnia
She is a cute kid
She supports Real Madrid
She likes looking at books
She loves the smell when my sister cooks
She likes singing when my sister's phone starts ringing
Her favourite colour is red
She likes being fed and going to bed
She is very smart
She like doing art
She is a very intelligent girl
She likes to do a twirl
She asks loads of questions
She likes doing suggestions
She likes watching TV
She likes to hide my house key
She likes hugging me
She likes climbing on a tree
She likes making a mess
She likes to guess
She likes everyone
When she is so happy she starts licking her tiny thumb
She is very creative
She loves all her relatives.

Iqra Sohail (11)

Lilly The Dog

Lilly is lovely,
Lilly is white,
Lilly is beautiful as the daylight.

When she raises from her bed,
You will know it is her,
Because she will climb on your head.

Chelsea Vidler (11)

My Sister

I would like to tell you about my sister
Her name is Annabel
For a very long time she hasn't been well
There have been lots of visits to hospitals
And many overnight stays
This causes interruptions
To her busy school days
I think she is amazing
As this year she has worked so hard
To get to school every day
Even though she suffers from a lot of pain
She still finds time to get good grades
She is my sister, the one who lives with me
A person with great responsibilities
Even though she is busy and has many things to do
She helps me with my homework and gets rid of the flu
She helps me when I'm down
And tells me not to frown
Even though sometimes we fight
But we can surely make up tonight
She is so great
She is such a good mate
My sister is one of a kind
And guess what? She is all mine!

Tara Rackham (11)

My Favourite Person

CS Lewis is an inspiration to young readers,
He makes his stories interesting when he writes,
He talks about the good and the bad.

He puts a lot of meanings into his stories,
His books have inspired me to be a writer,
That is why my favourite person of 2009
Is CS Lewis!

Jason Onyeje Ekejiuba (10)

30

My Sister

My sister's not my sister,
Some think this very strange,
When she's not around I miss her,
I hope she'll never change.
Sarah Pickett is her name,
My best friend is she,
Being happy is her game,
Bestest friends are we.
We're closer than close,
So sisters we are,
She's kinder than most,
Like a genie in a jar.
According to biology,
Sisters we are not,
But thinking logically,
We've been together since the cot.
So why's she so great?
Some people may ask,
Such a fabulous mate,
In glory she does bask.
We're such good friends,
Just me and her,
Together till the end,
Me and my sister.

Isla McLachlan (13)

My Amazing Dad

My dad is very good to me,
When he smiles he makes me feel like I'm in seventh heaven . . .

My dad makes me feel lovely and safe
When I am with him he shows me fun things to do
And makes my life better without a do.
When I see him go phew
The father I love is obviously the one and truly him.

Sade Thomas (11)

It's Hard To Say . . .

My favourite person is hard to say,
because I see all my family everyday,
when it comes to love and care,
I know my family will be there!
My mum is great and my best mate,
she's kind to us all and when she's around,
she always makes sure my frown is upside down!
My dad is also great and my best mate,
his jokes entertain me well,
just like he's cast a spell to draw our eyes on a big surprise he is to tell!
My brothers are cool and good fun,
they always pick on me,
but when they don't they won't mean to hurt a bee!
My sister's great and she's fun,
let's not forget she's number one!
My niece is cute and snappy,
but creates some stinky nappies!
My nan is nice, I love her lots and lots,
she's always there to love and care for my family!

So who should
it be?
Who's my favourite
person?

Samantha Jade Carmichael (10)

Alfie

A streak of brown and white, racing into the meadow,
We track his zig-zagging path through the deep green sea of swaying grass,
Energetic,
Content,
Later, beside the roaring fire, he snores gently,
Unaware of the world around him,
With hair as soft as silk and eyes of shimmering jewels,
That is Alfie.

Lucy Collier (12)

I Love You Dad!

Many poems have been written to explain,
How a mother's love can soothe the pain.
But little has been said about a father's concern,
So . . . now . . . I think it must be your turn.
A father's love for his off-spring,
Is just like that of a solid gold ring,
No matter what it is unending, never breaking,
Though . . . but sometimes bending.
His love is as strong as a mother's although . . .
Due to his personality, it sometimes doesn't show.
There is no love stronger, there is no love stronger, than that of a dad.
I love someone dearly (my dad).
Or of its lasting . . . however long.
He's kind as can be,
He makes me happy,
He's my dad, you see!
He takes me out to the park,
We play basketball and football,
He knows about everything.
I am so proud of him, and as I get bigger,
I just want to grow,
To be like my daddy,
'Cause I love him so!

Kristina Halili (10)

My Best Mother

You're a dependable source of comfort,
You're my cushion whenever I fall.
You help me when I am in trouble,
You'll always be there whenever I call.

I love you more than you know,
You have my total respect.
If I had a choice of lovely mothers,
You'd be the one I'd select.

Amir Ali (10)

33

My Favourite Person

Mia is my favourite person
She always makes me smile
She's my BFF, of course
And I would run a mile;
If ever she needed me.

Mia is my favourite person
We're always together at school
We always hang around each other
And everyone thinks it's cool.

Mia is my favourite person
We're always giving presents
We're always writing little notes
To us, there's nothing better.

Mia is my favourite person
And I know if I am sad
She will give me a great big hug
And say, 'Hey! Life's not that bad!'

Mia is my favourite person
At me she never shouts
We will always be BFFs
And I know we'll never fall out!

Emily-Rose Maule (9)

My Mum

My favourite person is my mum
'Cause I love the food she makes, like cookies, *yum!*
She is nice to me every day
So listen up to what I have to say.

My mum is kind to me
She taught me games, can't you see?
My mum is the best ever
Is there anyone better than her? I'd say, 'Never!'

Zakia Folson (9)

I Love My Sister

Isabel is so sweet
Like a chocolate treat
She loves to draw
And she is never a bore

She adores to write
And she's very bright
She is seven years old
And she is very bold

She is very upbeat
She dances on the balls of her feet
Isabel can stand on her hands
And when she's an author
She will have lots of fans

She is adorably cute
Like a ripe piece of fruit
And being a big sister I would say
When you're bored she will always come to play

She is the best sister
I could ever have asked for
And in my life, when she was born
It was like opening a new door.

Lauren Hopley (10)

My Favourite Person 2009

Miley is so smiley
With teeth that are so shiny
She turns into a rock star with one simple click
Miley is so smiley
With shoes that are so slick

Just
Like
Her!

Kasey Wall (11)

I Love My Grandma!

I love my grandma, so very much,
When I cried, she'd say, 'Hush, hush,'
Then she'd rock me on her lap,
Whilst I had a little nap,
That's why I love her so much!

I love my grandma, she is so smart,
We'd sit at the table and do some art,
So she'd get out the paints and brushes too
And it was always fun, cos I was with you!

When I got older, she taught me to cook,
Lots of foods . . . but not out of a book.
So as I prepared our Sunday dinner,
I always knew I was a winner,
A winner because,
I had a grandma who was,
Fun, kind, talented, caring and someone I loved so much!

So, as you can see,
My grandma to me,
Is a very special person,
She is the best, better than the rest . . .
That's why I love her so much!

Khaiya Rose (12)

Baby Bro

His eyes are like a shining star
It makes me giggle
His laugh is like a monkey
It makes me wiggle
But . . .
Runs faster than an energetic cheetah,
Scratches like a playful tiger
Most of all, his smile turns a frown
Upside down!

Abdul Sillah (11)

Homer Simpson

Homer Simpson;
An idiot in some people's minds,
But to me, he's an entertainer,
A one of a kind.
His fat posture,
His clumsy stance,
All contribute to his
Amusing appearance.
He lives in a town,
A town called Springfield,
You never know what
Troubles this setting will yield.
He likes drinking Duff Beer,
In fact, quite a lot,
He gets drunk and crawls home,
As if he's been shot.
His family consists of:
Bart, Lisa, Maggie and Marge,
There's never an agreement,
Between this family entourage.
Homer Simpson;
An idiot in some people's minds.

Charlie Farnham (13)

My Favourite Person

My favourite person of the year is, of course, my mum
My mum and I have such fun, in the shining sun!
She's always there, night and day, to help me when I'm stuck
She's like a charm of good luck.

If I put all the mums into one long line,
The only one who would stand out would, of course, be mine!
My mum is a lovely, cuddly lady,
With a great personality and a warm, fuzzy character
And that is why I love you Mum!

Charlotte Burnham (10)

My Friend

Do you want me to say
'I love you'
Or maybe whisper
'I need you'
I think the reason why
I say this to myself every night
Is because, 'I miss you'

Every time I see you pass by
Or you come to mine
There is always something
On my mind
That makes me want to ask
Why?

Are those hugs true
Or should I say
I don't want to
Cos I know that
It really hurts to
Make you mine
And be with me
All the time.

Leia Eaglestone (13)

Granny

My granny is the best
Better than my mum and all the rest.

She puts a smile on my face when I am down
And never tolerates a frown.

I almost see her every day
And she always wants to sing, dance or play.

She is the best granny a boy could ever have
Then I must be so lucky and so, so very glad!

Caolan Hay (10)

My Mum

My mum is the best from east to west
She is cool, fun and is the best out of the rest
We do things together in our fun way
We're always close, like two beans and we like going away
I like the snow and wind, Mum likes chills and sun
When I'm down and sad, my mum makes it fun.

She is the best and my hero
From 1.1 to zero
Happy, lonely, smart and sad
My mum rules and is never bad
Busy bees and silver fish
I'm so lucky to have my mum and I will never wish.

I like to go fishing, my mum likes the bay
I would rather be dozing every day
Blooming flowers, happy, not grey
Green grass, blue skies
Me and my mum like all pies
We have a dog who barks
Now and again I take him to parks
It's time to end, so read on
My mum's my hero, now say goodbye!

Chloe Jane Thomas (9)

My Mum!

She is always there for me,
Even if she's got stung by a bee,

She has always got something for me to do,
Even if it means taking my little sister to the loo!

She always helps me whenever I'm stuck
And while she's at it, she brings me luck,

She's the best! The best, favourite person of all
And that favourite person, is my mum!

Maisie Poulton (12)

My Favourite People

I have a bull mastiff called Rudy
Sometimes he can be very moody
He likes to be fussed
He thinks it's a must.

Ellie is my best friend
We will be friends till the end
She is blonde
And we have a strong bond.

Ethan is my baby brother
He thinks it would be funny to hide under a cover
Ethan's so cheeky
You would wish to meet him.

Last, but not least, is my dad
I guess he's not that bad
He can be embarrassing around my friends
He is just a big kid, but usually it's gardens he tends.

Sometimes I think
I'm lucky because
I haven't got one favourite person
I've got four!

Kayleigh Taylor (10)

My Mum Helps

My mum is special in every way,
She helps me every day,
If I fall, she'll comfort me,
Making sure I'm alright.
She helps me do my homework
And helps me day by day
And on stormy nights,
She'll tuck me up in bed
And chase my fears away.

Lauren Roxburgh (9)

My Cat, Meaka

My cat, Meaka, has the loudest of purrs
And the softest of fur
She doesn't really bite
And doesn't like to have a fight
She sits up there, on the fence
Casting her eye across the fields.

She likes to stride across our fence
But luckily, she doesn't get too tense
When she climbs up trees
It's obvious she's trying to flee.

She gets very excited
And even more delighted
When I stroke her
She makes the loudest purr.

She's got big, glaring, green eyes
She's has a very loud purr for someone of her size.

She loves to play with her toy snake
But once she starts to play, she doesn't take a break
She also doesn't like to take a bath
But when she has one, we all have a laugh.

Jazz Gordon (9)

She Is . . .

When I look at her hair
It reminds me of poppies flying in the wind.
When I look in her eyes
I see a raging sea.
When I smell her
It reminds me of a sweet-scented rose.
When I hear her voice
It makes me feel safe
She is my mum.

Freya Cicale-Brown (9)

My Grandpa

Age is but a number, a time, a date,
If he wants something now it's never too late,
A teacher so true, a heart of pure gold,
You are never too fat, too thin, young or old.

Behind the childish qualities I know,
Is a kind, wise man who never ceases to show,
His fears, his flaws, his talents and more,
None of which he'll apologise for!

A man of pride, but so humble too,
Knows just what to say, thinks everything through,
He's someone to confide in, whatever is wrong,
His words are a symphony, a heart-raising song.

He gives motivation without one second thought,
To him life's a lesson, we all need to be taught,
A hand you can hold, advice that you need,
Never shows any doubt, makes you ache to succeed.

From the bottom of my heart, the depths of my soul,
I thank you for helping me reach all my goals,
My dear Grandpa you show me light when it's dark,
I'll admire you always, you hold a place in my heart.

Emma Coleman (11)

My Favourite Person

She makes me happy in all kinds of ways,
Her smile is as sweet as ice cream,
Her hair is golden like a sunflower shining in the sun,
She comforts me when I am upset,
She never breaks a promise,
She keeps all my secrets and dreams safe,
I hope she will be there when I am older,
She is my best friend,
This person, is of course, my *mum!*

Ellie Marchant-Deadman (10)

My Favourite Person

It has to be my caring mother!
How could it possibly be any other?
She's as busy as a bee, morning till night,
Coping with her tasks with all her might.

The family has an early breakfast,
At school I don't want to arrive the last.
Baby brother throws a kiss from the car,
Whilst my sister and I wave from afar.

She always looks as pretty as a picture,
As she bends over and stirs the cake mixture.
The raisins in the bowl are golden dots,
Matching Mum's apron with its orange spots.

She sweeps and polishes to keep the house clean,
Until not a speck of dust is seen.
The garden attracts pedestrians' admiration,
For there's not a flower to beat Mum's carnation.

Yes! Mother is definitely my favourite person!
Without her the world would not go round!
She keeps all of the family safe and sound
And I wouldn't give her up for a billion pounds!

Adil Khan (11)

My Twin, Beth

There are a lot of people that I could write about,
But there is only one person who means so much to me,
My sister, my twin, my friend,
She's been there from the start,
She's never let me down and I doubt she ever will,
We have our fights, but soon get along great,
So, to sum it up, here are a few words that describe her:
Kind, funny, charming, cheeky and loving,
That's a few of the reasons why I'm proud to call her my twin, Beth!

Elena Jamison (11)

43

Super Grandad!

My grandad loves Milly his dog,
He even walks her in the fog!
Unfortunately on dogs I'm not too keen,
So when I visit he makes sure she can't be seen.

When I go to his home,
Around the garden he lets me roam,
Playing with him lots of sporty games,
Or dominoes inside if it rains!

Grandad sometimes comes for tea,
Which very much pleases me.
My favourite person is very clever,
So as a bank manager he was the best ever!

We go on trips,
And in the cafe, tea he sips,
But if we're having a lot of fun,
We might treat ourselves to a sticky bun.

My grandad is always there,
Getting ready to help and share,
Wishing me luck, cheering me on,
With him bad moments? I have none.

Charlotte Mellor (12)

My Favourite Person

The favourite person in my life
Is always there for me.
He helps me with my reading when I'm stuck,
He even took me camping and we stayed up all night long.
My favourite person is a soldier
Who always makes time for me.
My favourite person is . . .
Haven't you guessed yet?
It's . . . *Daddy!*

Blake Haddon (6)

My Favourite Person

Throughout the whole of my life,
I've met new people day by day.
Some make me laugh, some make me cry,
In many different ways.

First, there's my sister, Kathryn,
Who I look up to all the time.
She's very pretty and mostly fun
And always speaks her mind.

Next, there's my mum who keeps me safe
And shows me right from wrong.
She has a beautiful singing voice,
For singing her wonderful songs.

Last, there's my dad, who's big and strong,
Who helps me when I'm stuck.
He's strict, but kind and makes me laugh,
Whenever I'm down on my luck.

Out of all these people,
I don't know who would be
My favourite person, so instead,
I think I'll choose all three!

Sarah Hainey (11)

My Friends

My friends,
Are one of a kind.
They cheer you up,
When you are down.
They make you happy,
All the time.
We laugh and cry
And laugh some more,
Because we are best friends!

Charlie Taylor (12)

My Best Friend

My best mate,
Is no human,
But she's there whatever the date
And this is why she's so great!

She's fast and understanding,
She's kind, but slightly strange,
She's nearly always daring,
But is normally very dazed.

She's funny and she's loveable,
She's smart and well-behaved,
She is cute and so, so huggable
And always cheers me up.

Crazy and always pretty,
She's the twin I never had!
But she can't hug me, it's a pity,
Because she's really, really soft.

Furry, cuddly and always hungry,
My best friend's name is Meg
And no, she's not a human,
She's a red and white Staffie instead!

Katie Allick (9)

Not CFC Free

C razy like my dog, Meg
H appy all the time
A lways having fun
R unning down the hill
L oving Meg all the time
O pening ideas all the time
T alking about weird stuff a lot
T iming how fast I can run
E ating lots and lots of Jaffa Cakes!

Eilidh Catriona Scott (9)

My Mum

My mum is very special,
She's very sweet to me,
And when I'm down in the dumps,
She's always there for me.

She's always very funny,
We love her when she laughs,
She smells as sweet as honey,
And she loves a boiling bath.

Nothing's ever boring,
When Mummy is around,
She helps us with our drawing,
Pencils working is the only sound.

We sometimes call her Glamour Girl,
As she walks down the stairs,
She likes this comment very much,
And all our admiring stares,

My mum is very special,
She's very sweet to me,
And when I'm down in the dumps,
She's always there for me.

Lauren Sergi (10)

My Friend

I walk to school with her each day
We chitter-chatter on the way
When we get there we meet some boys
We read some books and play with toys
The teacher calls us into school
So we put away the books and ball
At the end of lessons we must go
On the way home my friend and I
We are so happy, we could cry!

Jazzmin Spencer (9)

My Friends

My friends are the greatest
My friends are the best
They always know when I'm upset
They're better than the rest.

Hannah is the funniest
She always makes me laugh
She's caring, kind and much, much more
She gave me her pink scarf.

Abbie is an angel
She likes to wear a skirt
She always, always cares for me
Especially when I'm hurt.

So now we're in Year 6
It's time to say goodbye
I know that I will miss them both
But I'll try not to cry!

My friends are the greatest
My friends are the best
They always know when I'm upset
They're better than the rest!

Charlotte Fellows (10)

My Mum Is Amazing

My mum's eyes twinkle like the stars in the sky
My mum's hair is black as it shines in the sunlight
My mum's lips are as pink as pink petals
My mum wears diamond jewellery all over
My mum wears silky scarves as soft as cotton
My mum's eyelashes are as big as a snip of hair
My mum's cheeks are as red as a rose
My mum wears designer long cloaks, like a model
My mum is amazing!

Humairaa Iqbal (9)

My Favourite Person

I'm going to write about two people,
Not any family or friends that I have now.
Eventually I will meet them
Someday, and somehow.

My sister and my auntie are having baby boys
Hip, hips and hoorays.
They both are coming in November
That will be two special days.

I can't wait till they come
The babies and I will be so happy.
Cuddling and playing
I'll even help change their nappies!

One boy on the eighteenth
And the other on Bonfire Night.
Two little boys soon will be playing
I hope they do not fight.

I told you all I can for now
And all I'm able to say.
But I'm hoping by this time next year
Two little girls will be on their way!

Joanna Marie Thomas (9)

Dad

My favourite person is my dad
He is always there when I'm sad
We always have a laugh
And go on bike rides over the park
He plays games with me like snakes and ladders
And absolutely loves the Hammers
He has embarrassed me a couple of times
Including at school when it's home time
He is the best dad anyone could have!

Emily James (10)

Mummy

My favourite person is my mummy,
I love her all the time,
Even when I'm in trouble
For telling a little lie.

A love that cannot be broken, never,
A bond that will last a lifetime, forever,
A friendship that cannot be broken, ever
A hug from you and me.

Tears from her eyes should be wiped away,
For what I have to say:
She's always there for me,
When I'm sick and in sorrow.
One to two, two to three,
She's the best, but not all mine.
She's says I'm crazy, I don't care
I'm annoying all the time.
But best of all, I love my mum
And she loves me, although
We all love our mums in a way.

'Sleep well.'

Kara Allen (10)

Alexandra

Alexandra is so sweet and loves to say, *'Tweet'!*
She is always making me laugh, by making funny stuff
She is so very kind and is always on time and never behind
Alexandra always giggles and sometimes fiddles
She loves to go on a course, because she can't ride a horse
Alex loves reading a book and always says, 'Look!'
She loves eating cake, but hates to bake
She plays the electric guitar just like a night-time star
My dear, no need to frown when you're feeling down
Alexandra, my dear friend, it's time for the poem to end!

Yasmin Alsaady (8)

All My Favourite People

My mum, my mum,
Gives us all her love,
And big, lovely warm hugs.
Alan, Alan,
Has an Audi,
Driving it around all proudly.
Sarah and Rachel,
Are going to uni,
However they don't like the Goonies.
Suzie and Chloe,
Like to have fun,
Especially when we run.
Hank hamster, Hank hamster,
When he nibbles his ladder,
It doesn't affect his bladder.
Casper and Mickey (kittens),
Are always fighting,
And biting.
Missy cat, Missy cat,
When she's jumping around,
She never gets down.

Daniel Taylor (11)

My Mum

My favourite person is my mum
Because she always cares even if I'm a pain.
My mum does everything for me
And anything I need help with.
My mum is my life
And as long as she's alive, my life is worthwhile.

As I said, my mum is my life,
She means the world to me.
With her around, my life is going to be wild
And packed full of stuff that I know is going to be full of fun.

Lauren Hawthorne (9)

The Mum I Love

My mum is a good'en,
She looks after me,
She might even moan and groan at me,
My mum makes me tidy my room,
She makes me do chores,
She is the one I love!
My mum is pretty,
She also smells good too,
My friends say she's a model,
Her hair is all nice and curly,
That's my lovely mum,
My mum cooks me yummy food,
She gives me dazzling cash,
She buys my beautiful clothes,
My mum gives me a warm welcoming home,
That's why I love her!
My mum is the one I can talk to,
She is the one I trust,
My mum tells me the truth,
Even if it hurts!
That's the mum I love!

Lauren Sonia Campbell (10)

My Favourite Person - Family

My favourite people are my mum and dad
Cos they help me when I'm sad.

My gran and grandad too
Cos they are there for me when I am blue.

My big brother is mad
But he loves me so much it makes me glad.

But all and all I love them all
Cos through and through
They love me, they love me true!

Kelly Larmour (11)

My Favourite Person

You are my favourite person
On this whole world.

Why . . . ?

When my mum wasn't with me,
You looked after me.
When I was sick,
You did everything for me
To make me better,
For this, I love you.

You always supported me,
Even when I did naughty things.
You did a lovely dinner,
When I felt hungry,
For this, I love you.

You are in my heart and mind,
Even though we are not close together.
You are the only special one to me,
You are the person who helps me
And you are my *grandmother!*

Ruwaydah Azad (6)

My Dog, Saffi

She always likes cuddles,
But doesn't like puddles!

She likes to go on walks,
But don't let her off her lead; she may not get her daily feed!

The best thing about my dog, Saffi,
Is that she's not tough or rough,
She is cuddly remember, not puddly.

The best thing is . . .
She is my dog, Saffi!

Erin Clayton (10)

Maggie 'N' Kate

I started my time at Balby Carr
But with my attitude, I knew I wouldn't get far
But then I met Kate
And we became great mates
We could tell each other secrets, young and old
But all of them were never to be told.

But Kate grew old and had to go
So who was I gonna tell my secrets to now . . .

Then along came Maggie who told me the news
That she was the one I could turn to
To wash away my blues!

I didn't think I'd like her
Cos it wouldn't feel the same
But then I grew to like her
I even liked her name!

So, my two favourite people are
Maggie and Kate
Who'll always remember
And never forget!

Shannon Hancox (12)

My Friend, Bingo

I cannot wait for the school day to end,
To get back home to my wee friend,
He's white and cuddly and round and stout,
When you talk to him you have to shout.
Bingo only has one ear,
Which makes it hard for him to hear,
If I'm not looking over the wall for him,
He'll baa and baa as I appear,
He really is my special friend
And I know I'll love him to the end.

Aaron McMullin (9)

Lyndsay

My favourite person is called Lyndsay
We are happy every day
Together we have lots of fun
In the countryside, in the summer sun
We love dogs, big or small
Jumping over the garden wall
In Scotland there is a lot of rain
Pattering down the neighbour's drain
But that doesn't bother us at all
Having fun with a bouncy ball!

In school, we work very hard
We make decorations from paper, glue, scissors and card
We like maths, reading, writing and lots more
When we are finished, our heads and hands are very sore
When we've done so much work, we feel tired
But surely we should be admired!
In the playground, we like to run, hop, skip and jump
And sometimes we land with a great big *thump!*
My favourite person, Lyndsay, is very clever
Being the best of friends, *forever!*

Amy Gatherer (9)

My Mum

She is the kindest person, my mum
She shows me what to do to keep me safe and sound
She gives me lots of special hugs, in her loving arms
She smiles, which lights up my day, whether I'm happy or sad
She is always the one I look forward to seeing when I run out of school
She makes me feel so special, with her kind and loving words
She tucks me up in bed at night and gently kisses my head
She is my mum and always will be my very special friend
She loves me and I love her, more than words can say
She is my very favourite person in the whole wide world
That's my mum!

Charlotte Wortley (8)

Ruth, My Best Friend

You are like a flower,
A rose to be exact,
Or maybe like a brand new gate,
That never comes unlatched.
You understand my worries
And listen to my dreams,
You listen to how I feel about life
And know what it all means.

All the times we argue and fight,
I then feel bad and have a lot of pain,
I know inside it isn't right,
It feels that I've fallen from the sky, like the rain.

You are like an owl,
Both beautiful and wise,
Or like a friendly ghost,
Whose spirit never dies.

I always think of all the good times that we've been through,
I love you, Ruth, with all my heart,
This poem, I dedicate to you.

Joanna Priya Chandra (11)

My Favourite Person - God

Sometimes I think to myself
Is God really real?
But then I think, *don't be stupid,*
God is great!
If God were a planet, He would be Jupiter, the greatest of them all
The rhythm of His name is peace and equality
God is like an old eagle owl
Full of knowledge and kindness
God is like us humans, He is everywhere looking over us
God is in many different forms, like Allah or just God
He has helped us to keep peace and the last hope of happiness.

Oliver Keyser (13)

My Mum

Mummy, thank you
You are my mum
Mummy, you're the best
Mummy, you are loving.

You are my sunshine
And I love you!
You are so lovely
And you are so kind,
My colourful mummy,
I'm so glad you are mine.

Look at me and then you will see
Just how good my mum has been
Over the years you love me more each day
Even when I'm bad, your love still stays the same.

You are always with me
And everyone can see
Just how much I love you
And you love me
So, Mummy, thank you for loving me.

Alice Jacqueline Hitching (11)

My Favourite Pet Is . . .

My favourite pet is Barney, the dog,
He jumps like a kangaroo,
When he's having fun with you,
He's always cuddly even when his nose is runny,
He's cute and lovely, even though his fur is scruffy,
He's very fast at running and likes to lick your face
And can always beat you at every race,
He's small and hyper and likes his belly tickled,
He loves to play games and have a little nibble,
Barney is the best dog ever and I can prove it too,
That he's the number one star and will always stand by you.

Megan Sharp (11)

My Best Friend, Merin!

My best friend,
Will last till the end,
How wonderful!

Merin is her name,
She is full of flame,
How wonderful!

How bossy can she be?
Hopefully not like a buzzing bee (*bzzz*)
How wonderful!

They call her merry,
Because she loves berries,
How wonderful!

She is tall,
Unlike a ball,
How wonderful!

She is very nice,
Just like mice,
How wonderful!

Harleen Singh (10)

My Nice Mum

M is for Mum
Y is for young

N is for nice
I is for independent
C is for caring
E is for everlasting love

M is for marvellous
U is for understanding
M is for magnificent

  My mum!

Grace Easlea (9)

Jane, My Godmother

On days when I go to Jane's house,
I'm all shy,
I never speak,
I'm like a mouse!

On days when I go to Jane's flat,
We make bracelets,
Necklaces
And have fun like that!

On days when I go to Jane's mansion,
We sing,
Dance
And talk about fashion!

Jane is very, very funny,
When she is,
It hurts my tummy!

Me and Jane are good together,
We love each other
And it will be like that *forever!*

Hansine Marshall (10)

Jet

Jet is my cute little kitten,
Though you'll dread to be bitten.

His fur is black and his whiskers are white,
To see him will be love at first sight.

Sometimes he's calm and quiet,
But more often than not, he makes a big riot!

He is jet-black, he is jet-fast!
He loves attention and needs affection.

I love him very much,
My beautiful, black cat!

Eleanor Coyne (9)

My Friend Monty

Monty is my very best friend
Fluffy and white, cheerful and bright
And I think about my friend Monty
Day and night.

He twitches his fleecy little nose
He snuffles and sniffles wherever he goes
And my cunning little friend
Chews the carpet from end to end.

Monty loves his food
And to have his bowl in a certain place
Dandelions are the best
Bringing a grin to his furry face.

My lovely Monty-Boy
Brings me such sweet joy
And I love him really
With all the cuddles he gives dearly.

Monty makes my atmosphere sunny
My Monty is a wonderful bunny.

Sarah Prentice (10)

Sammy, Sammy, Sammy

Sammy is my cat
I've very sure of that.

He likes to jump and dance
It sends me in a trance.

He's my very furry mate
He is always very great.

Without Sammy I would be very lost
To lose him would be such a big cost.

But that will never happen, because I love him so
He loves me back, so he will never go!

Connie Corden (9)

My Big But Little Surprise

I was waiting for that, 8 and nearly 9 years before it happened.
But finally it did,
I was in the car driving to hospital with my dad,
to see my mum, with someone I'd never met before.
That became my favourite person.
We got out the car, and in the doors,
And it was the time I saw them.
My mum holding him.
My tiny brother.
From that first instance I knew he was going to be special for me.
I never thought something as amazing like that could happen,
but now I know that it can.
It was a surprise for all of the family,
but I took that day into the middle of my heart.
We went home.
I went to bed but I didn't sleep the whole night!
'Cause I was thinking, how happy I was going to be for the rest of my life.
And from that time I have never been wrong!

Lots of love to my little brother Wiktor/Victor.

Karolina Sepiak (9)

A Fabulous Friend

I have an amazing friend
She goes with me round the bend
Up and down, left to right
Always there when I'm in a fright
She'll always help me find my way
Almost every single day
She will always care
And will help me find what to wear
If she wasn't there
My life would be bare
Best friends stick together
In every weather!

Ellie Carter (10)

My Dog, Roxie

My dog, Roxie,
A happy thing,
A thing of love and care,
Her tail wagging all day long,
She's a friend who is always there.

Our adventures are great,
Always fun,
On the run,
Under the table,
Keeping away from Mum.

Out for a walk,
Bouncing along,
Holding her head,
Wow, she's strong!

Home at last,
Roxie falls asleep,
Dreaming of streams
And doggy things.

Sophie Dennison (8)

Raven

My dog is just like a raven, black all over
She is all bark and no bite
But sometimes she and my other dog get into a fight
My dog has eaten just about everything
From socks to her own waste
But I have to admit, I was quite scared
When we first came face to face!
She is just like a mole, because in the garden
She digs lots of holes
She is just like a meerkat when she stands on her hind legs
But at night, in front of the fire, she puts her claws away
And cuddles up with me, until the next day.

Lucy Irvine (11)

Hollie

My favourite person
Is my best friend
We do everything together
She's ten years old
And full of fun
Her antics are a hoot
We laugh, we skip
We run and jump
We're always playing around
When our mothers call us
For our food
We never can be found
My friend is really
Great to know
And she is very jolly
I love my best friend
Very much
My best friend's name is
Hollie!

Angharad Cayford (10)

My Special Mum

My mum is . . . my unique treasure,
Her heart glistens in the enchanting moonlight.
My mum is . . . my hero and inspiration,
She is considerate, humble, modest and loyal,
My mum would do anything to provide for me and my brother.

My mum is . . . someone I could look up to, as well as to say,
That I'm proud to have a mum like you!
My mum gives me the courage to stand up to the bullies
And never give up,
Moreover, to fight with justice, because she is always there for me.
My mum is a beautiful opal and this poem proves it,
Thank you, Mum, for your devotion and also your affection.

Achaia Hinds (12)

My Favourite Person

My favourite person is someone who sews my skirts so neat,
Whether it is plain or whether it has pleats.
My favourite person is someone who looks after me when I am ill,
Even if they don't want to, they will.
This person hates the noise, this person hates to cook,
But gets a little over-excited when she reads a book.
The characters come alive and run fast beside her,
But she suddenly stops when the cat starts to purr.
This person finds science interesting, even if I do not
I think chocolate is fabulous, she hates the lot.
I love this person, even though we have little in common,
I like to do plaits and she likes to do buns.
This person likes all the colours of the rainbow, just like me
And we both like going to be beach and standing in the sea.
I wonder if you have guessed my favourite person of interest,
Sometimes she thinks I am lovely and sometimes she thinks I am a pest.
If you are still thinking of who this person could be,
Stop, look, listen and read and find out who it is,
Of course, it's my lovely, snuggly, bubbly, cuddly *mum!*

Radeyah Anjum (11)

My Favourite Person Is My Rabbit

My favourite person is my rabbit, Hartley Hazelnut Diggums,
He hops around and shivers, but he never quivers,
He looks like Peter Rabbit, he only needs a little blue jacket,
I hold him in my arms, as I slide down the slide,
That's his little theme park ride.

We've only had him for a week,
But what a joy it is to speak,
About my little rabbit,
I don't like getting out of bed,
But Hartley's always in my head,
So I run downstairs as quick as I can,
To see my darling little man.

Georgia Rose (9)

A Golden Heart

Her heart of pure gold
Her eyes shine with love
She is always there to help me
Give me love and hope
A warm smile is always on her face
That is what gives me strength
'Mother' is a word that means the world to me
And is the sweetest in the world
She fills my days with love
Sweet dreams and bedtime stories
A kiss to take away my fears
She is always there to wipe my tears
She gave me the gift of life
Thank you for all your care and love
And all the long hours you've spent
Praying for God to bless me
Thank you for all the countless things you have done
Thank you for all the little things you give
Throughout each busy day.

Serene Khabbass (11)

You Are My Favourite Person!

You, reader, are my favourite person. Why?
Because think of all the things you could be doing now . . .

Writing sonnets, tying bonnets,
Digging holes, studying moles,
Playing with toys, using Game Boys,
Watching DVDs, catching Frisbees,
Vacuuming your room, experimenting - *boom!*
Reading 'The Big Green Poetry Machine', in which all the poets are keen!
In there, flip to page 81, as you read my poem, you'll have so much fun!
You, reader, are my new friend, 'cause look at that, you've reached the end!
Now run along, I've used enough time
And remember, you are my favourite person 2009!

Nicole Hogan (11)

Our Dog, Tess

I'm going to tell you about our dog, Tess
And how she makes my mum stressed.

She has a very deep bark
And her fur is very dark.

When she's happy, she wags her tail,
A bit like a ship's sail.

When she is in the mood,
She will eat all our food.

She is quite big,
About the size of a pig!

When she sees us at the gate,
She knows that she is late.

If you have treats,
You can feel her heart beat.

So, that's all you need to know about Tess,
Except you should know you have to clean up her mess!

Jamie Herbert (10)

Untitled

This is a tribute,
To my Alaskan malamute,
He is a daft playsuit,
Who bounces like he's wearing a jumpsuit,
No one will substitute my Alaskan malamute.

My Alaskan malamute's name is Malaki,
He is my kind of special guy,
Who loves all kinds of pies, and chasing flies,
He never makes me cry,
But he does make me sigh,
As he's always on a high,
Now it's time to say bye.

Kelsey-Lee Wright (11)

Best Buddies

Strength beyond belief
Not frightened of the dark
Or my little brother
Actually, I think
We were meant for one another.

When I am tired
He helps me get to sleep
Apart from when the TV is blaring on and on
He never shouts at me
Or tells me off
And when we fight
He never hurts me
Even though he's strong.

You are probably thinking
That it's my dad
Oh no, you are so wrong
Did I mention it is my ted
And I have had him for so long?

Harvey Wolstencroft (10)

Who Is She?

Not being too loud,
She stands out from the crowd.
Always being the smallest,
She somehow is trying to be the tallest.

Even when she is in pain,
She's always ready for another game.
I love it when she's always there,
Even when she's waiting by my chair.

Even when I get the blame,
She always feels the same.

So I'm happy to be her older sister!

Kavita Virdee (11)

My Grandpa

My grandpa means a lot to me
And if you read this you will see.
Sometimes I think he's solar-powered,
By day he's active, at night he's tired.

My grandpa has grey hair -
Well, what's left of it up there!
Glasses perched on the end of his nose,
Reading the paper, he begins to doze.

My grandpa likes anything sweet,
That's cakes, chocolates and sugary treats.
And if you need proof,
Well, he has only got one tooth!

My grandpa loves walking
And it's the same for talking.
I've heard all of his stories by now
And sometimes I wonder, how?

It's because I spend so much time with him!

Sam Wright (12)

My Friend, Grace

My friend, Grace,
Is a disgrace,
As she never takes a bath.

She dances about like a clown
And always wears a funky crown.

She is very, very smelly
And loves to eat jelly.

Yep, that's my friend, Grace,
A very big disgrace.

But all that matters in the end,
Is that Grace is my favourite friend!

Fatimah Khawaja (9)

68

My Dad

Even though he shouts a lot,
he is always there for me,
he is always looking to see if I'm sad,
for a chance to make me happy.

Whenever I'm down or feeling blue,
he's always got to see if I'm okay,
because he loves me,
hip hip hooray.

Even when I'm annoyed with him,
he always makes me smile,
I don't know why he does this though,
it can make me run a mile.

I really, really love my dad,
he's always warm and true,
and someday I hope you will understand dad,
that *I love you!*

Love Satya.

Satya Ram Kissun (11)

Untitled

Will is my brother who I love very much,

He is funny,
He smells so yummy,
He gives good cuddles,
He jumps in puddles,

We have lots of fun,

He makes us laugh,
He loves to dance,
He wears a nappy,
He is so happy,

My little brother is a number one baby!

Olivia Jayne Tideswell (6)

Auntie Lesley

Only nine years ago, standing by my side,
Vowing to help me be welcomed into the church,
One of my godparents, a family friend,
Who will be forever.

Just seven years ago, holding me close,
Smiling in a picture frame,
Though I was looking clueless.

Just over three years ago,
Walking along, with her and my mum,
At the 'Race for Life', only we were doing it for her.

Just one month ago,
Only me and my mum doing the 'Race for Life',
For the third time, still for her,
Even though this year she wasn't with us.

Today, my mum, not me, and my dad
At her funeral,
My lovely godmother, Lesley, now in Heaven.

Annabel Eira Morgan (9)

My Favourite Person

My favourite person is my baby brother,
He is so unusual, he's like no other.

He is so cute, he makes me laugh,
We are always together, we couldn't be apart.

We play together from dusk till dawn,
I am so glad my baby brother was born.

People say we look alike, that we're the spit of each other,
I am proud of that and I say, 'Yes, that's my baby brother!'

I will always be there for him, because he's my brother,
We look forward to growing up together,
We will look out for each other.

Daisy-May Palmer (10)

My Favourite Person Is My Grandad

He's really, really great,
On Saturday he takes me to the park,
Where we play football till late.

He thinks he's Freddy Flintoff,
Spinning that corky with tricks,
Trying to bowl me out all day,
But still can't hit those sticks.

Then there's my CDs,
Which he puts up with for me,
As he drives along and tries to sing the songs,
But it always sounds funny to me.

My grandad bought a bike this year,
I thought he was too old,
But the speed he goes,
And the way his hair blows,
It just goes to show you're never too old.

He's just a big kid!

Lewis Saunders (11)

Scarlet Rose, My Baby Sister

The night she came, I will always remember
The snow lay deep on that cold December
From the day she came home, I have never felt alone
The shadow that is my baby sister

She smiles, she laughs, she giggles at me
And usually, she eats all of my tea!

Some mornings she wakes me up with a slap on the cheek
And then she wants me to play hide-and-seek
But she never realises that I always peep
When we play hide-and-seek

Oh, I'm glad I have my little baby sister.

Louis Parr (10)

My Mum

My favourite person is my mum,
If I need her for something, she will come,
She's beautiful, kind and clever,
I will definitely love her forever.

My mum is very cool,
She'll walk me there and back from school,
I'll tell you why she stands out from all the other mums in the playground,
It's because she has glossy hair, just like a Hollywood star, she's great to have around.

My mum is very skilled,
She does tennis, swimming and athletics, which makes me really thrilled,
She can also play the piano and viola,
And her job's a property solicitor.

My favourite person is my mum,
If I need her for something, she will come,
She's amazing fun to have around,
I know she'll keep my feet on the ground.

Emily Geen (10)

My Sister

My sister is so cool,
But she is not a fool.

My sister is so funky,
But she is not a monkey.

My sister is so nice,
But she is not a lice.

My sister really loves me,
But she also loves her tea.

My sister gives the best hugs
And I really love her fluffy rug.

She is my sister!

Samantha May Hubbard (10)

72

My Dog, Lucky

My dog, Lucky, is the best
With her short-cut ears she beats the rest
She is brown and white and black
She has tiger stripes down her back
She has a tail with a little white tip
And her cute paws have a white dip.

My dog, Lucky, is a really special dog
She is sweet and smart, but eats like a hog
When I'm happy, she's yappy and runs around the street,
When I'm sad, she's mad and slumps at my feet.

My dog, Lucky, knows all the tricks
But she's not so good at fetching sticks
Every day she looks so cute
It just sends your heart a-shoot.

This is why Lucky is my favourite pet in the world
We are friends forever
We will love each other whatever.

Emma Godfrey (12)

Uncle C

I saw him for the last time that day,
I cried and I had to say missing you will be tough.
Without you Uncle C, life will be rough,
But I want to remember you and me having fun,
Playing in the park, under the sun.
We'd put our fingers in the fish tank
And throw some food in and wait until it sank.
At your wedding, I was a flower girl,
My dress was lovely and pretty, I felt on top of the world.
I miss you, Uncle C,
But you will somehow always be with me,
I wish I could see you now,
I just wonder, how!

Madeleine McDowell (11)

My Favourite Person

My favourite person
My favourite person
Is Rish, Rishona is her name
She's my big cousin
I love her all the same.

We talk on the phone
Because she lives far away
She likes laptops, I like singing
But it doesn't matter because we're just cousins.

She's proud to be black
I am too
She's funny and kind, has sparkling eyes
Brilliant, clever and wise, wise like an owl
She's just like a big sister to me
She creates a great atmosphere.

Rishona is a 1st rate role model to me
That's why she's my favourite person.

Sahyna McPherson (10)

My Mummy Is Funny!

My mummy is very funny
I spent nine months in her tummy
At Easter, she runs about the house dressed as a bunny
On Hallowe'en, she is a witch with a cat
And she eats all my treats and gets very fat
She is Mrs Claus at Christmas
Sometimes threatening to give me coal
I look at her and say
'How can you be Mrs Claus? She's in the North Pole!'
My mummy is very funny when she dances and sings
And whilst she is doing that, I count all her many shiny rings
I love my mummy, she is great
I love watching TV, so tonight I hope she lets me stay up late!

Kiera Joanna Jones (8)

Best Friends Forever

There is one person who is always there,
Anytime, anyplace, anywhere;
My life is full of ups and downs,
Quite the same with smiles and frowns.

Thea is the name of my dearest friend,
She is always happy to give and lend -
Caring, reliable and ever so passionate . . .
So many a-message I will send!

The time we spend together – so careless ever so fun,
But, when she leaves, the flame of hope flickers to see her
once more,
To be free with each other, or work at that difficult sum,
The flame is ignited again, the second she walks in the door . . .

Such good times we spend together,
In all different ways, in all sorts of weather,
So now to conclude this poem by dedicating it to Thea!
Thea! You are the best friend I can have . . . ever.

Emily Chen (10)

My Mother

You are the sea to me
Clear, deep and always moving
You are a flower to me
Blossoming, beautiful and natural
You are my life
The reason I am here is because of you
And I loved you, love you and always will love you
You are the heart of a fire
Warm, loving and always growing
You are a curry
Spicy, colourful and endeavouring
My mother is unique to me
Because she is mine and always will be.

Murshed Ahmed (10)

My Grandad!

You're not just my grandad you're my best friend.
All the memories we have shared I will keep locked away.
I want you to know I will never forget you.
If I was to choose who would live or die I would give my life for you.
I'm 13 years old and I can honestly say
no one in the whole world can lead me straight except you.
We have our arguments about the most stupid thing.
I can't stand us falling out.
I see things that are indescribable for the human eye,
you lead me to the most unremarkable places.
We have had so many adventures shared that will never
be forgotten as long as I live.
When I grow up I want my grandchild to have friendship like
I have with you.
You're my grandad, my best friend, my pal, my mate, my idol,
and I want you to know I want to be like you when I grow up,
achieve so many things.
Thank you for giving me that chance.

Jessica Wrightman (13)

David Bautista

D avid Bautista is his name
A nd WWE is his game
V ery good at doing his part
I s enduring pain on his partner's behalf
D oes not back down from *any* challenge

B ack from injury
A bout four months out
U gly anger brewing inside him
T opping his standard every time
I n the best way he can
S urprising everyone by what he achieves
T ime, time and time again
A lways will he be my favourite person.

Courtney Kirk (11)

Number One Grandma

Sparkly eyes, curly hair, glasses that need cleaning!
Gets down on the floor and can't get up,
I need to help her, she gets stuck!
She often forgets things,
But she never forgets to tell me how much she loves me!
My grandma is far more special to me than anyone on Earth,
She is really so wonderful,
I tell her every day that I love her so much that I just can't explain!
She lets me stick up all my pictures on her kitchen wall,
She never throws my drawings out, she always keeps them all!
She's loving, patient,
She's caring and kind,
She will always be one of a kind!
If all the grandmas in the world stood in a line,
The number one grandma would be mine, every time!
I couldn't bear to be without her,
She's always by my side,
That's why my grandma's the best and will be all my life!

Claudia Wilkes-Brough (10)

My Best Friend

My best friend is my uncle
I call him Uncle Pearce
We go fishing at the river
To catch some salmon or trout
It is very funny to get them out
Because they wiggle about.

He is my mother's brother
And he is very good at pool
He showed me how to play and aim the cue
He has a little red car
It takes him very far
He drives to work and home again
Even when it starts to rain.

Lee McCullagh (7)

My Dog, Max

I have lots of favourite people, the list just does not end,
So my poem will be about my favourite furry friend.
His name is Max and he is a dog,
He is crazy, mad and jumps like a frog.
When he gets bored, he gets really silly
And he loves playing with my best friend's dog, Milly.
He is a Lab-Collie cross,
But to me, he's better than candyfloss.
When I take him for walks, we have so much fun,
Except when he sees a cat, then it's *run, run, run!*
His sense of smell is like a thousand noses,
But he prefers fox poo to a bunch of roses!
When we have dinner, he sits at my feet,
Waiting for anything that falls to eat.
He chews on the furniture, he rips up the floor,
He barks at the postman, more and more.
He chases the cats and digs up the ground,
But to me he's worth more than a million pounds!

Bianca Ballingall (11)

My Dad

He goes to work in the morning,
Comes home and says, 'Goodnight,'
My dad is always there for me,
With a smile that spells delight,
He is such a funny man,
Is playful and very proud.

You're always there to make me laugh,
You, me, Mum and Tag,
We're such a happy family,
Every moment is filled with joy,
Laughter, fun and happiness,
Thanks again for being my dad
Because you're the best anyone could have!

Benn Swift (11)

Waiting

Every day I sit there thinking,
Waiting for someone to be there, to comfort me,
This long wait seems like it's going to be
A never-ending experience.
Nearly everybody I talk to has that hatred for me,
It's OK, I'm still waiting.
They say everything is for a time,
But I'm still waiting for an end.
I talk to specialists, but they can't specify on my feelings.
Waiting, I ask a teacher for help,
But they don't understand my feelings . . .
Well, that's what I think.
I come home from school, I don't get a greeting,
I go to my room, still nothing,
I was sleeping and an angel came to me,
It seemed like it wasn't true,
But yes, *God* answered my prayers and took away my misery,
I found my favourite person is . . . me.

Aaron Chen (12)

How I Feel About My Friend

My friend is kind and charming
He is always on the move
I will always be his friend, always.

He is gifted
He never messes about with others
And is always there to play with you.

This is how my friend is like . . .
This is how a jolly good friend of mine should be like
This is how a jolly good friend should be like
And should stay like that forever!

And I think my friend thinks about me like this and I like that
And this is how me and my friend make more friends and they like us.

Azhar Karmalkar (10)

Always There

From Primary one,
Through rain and sun,
You've been there.
Good and bad,
Happy and sad,
You've been there.
You said no way,
But you moved away,
But you were still there.
You're moving here,
So you'll be near,
And you'll be there.
Off to school,
And you'll look cool,
But for me you'll be there.
Through the time,
You'll be mine,
My one special person.

Alexis O'Reilly (11)

I Love My Mum

She is the sunlight in my day
I give her flowers in spring bank May
She is the tree I lean upon
She is the one that makes bad things be gone
She is the words inside my song
And I love her, because she's my mum
She is the one who knows me best
She is the bird feeding me in my nest
She is the one who cares for me
She is the eyes that help me see
She is the person who tells me what's wrong
She is the words inside my song
And I love her, because she's my mum!

Dewi Evans (9)

My Favourite Person

M y favourite person is lots of fun
Y es, she is my sister but also my chum

F rom time to time we engage in a fight
A nd we swing our fists with all our might
V ictory is sweet but it always turns out alright
O ften we play voyages through space or sing like superstars all night
U nder the table we build a tent for two
R ain or sun we find something to do
I do my homework but she does not
T elevision hits her spot
E ven though we are different I love her a lot

P laystation is her favourite stop
E veryone thinks that she should have a shot at
R eading and writing and cleaning her room, or
S crubbing and polishing or sweeping with a broom
O ften she will leave her clothes on the floor
' N aughty girl!' my mum shouts – but life would be dull without Sasha about.

Ciara Barrett (10)

Mum

I thank her for the confidence she has given me in becoming
an independent boy
She has always shown me the true meaning of an ideal child
Because of her, I never felt the need to keep my head down
I thank her for the sacrifices that she still continues to make for me
I thank her for all that she is doing in order to build a brighter tomorrow for me
I love you, Mum
You are always there to help me
You are always there to guide me
You are always there to laugh with me
You are always there to cry with me
But most important, you are always there to love me
And I want to assure you that I am always there to love you too.

Jeet Dave (9)

My Favourite Person

A poem for my sister Alex.

I have a big sister Alex,
She's pretty and very tall!
She takes me to the cinema,
But prefers to go to the ball!

I have a big sister Alex,
She babysits and lets me eat crisps!
She lets me stay up late and listen to her music discs!

I have a big sister Alex,
She loves to party in pink!
All the boys think she's gorgeous,
And often give her a wink!

I have a big sister Alex,
I think she's really quite funny,
I'd love to be like her when I grow up,
Because I think she's as sweet as honey!

Leah Nicholson (11)

My Little Sister, Daa-Daa

I've got this little sister, Daa-Daa . . .
She is just only two
And her favourite animals
Do go *moo!*

My sister is so sweet
And so say all she meets.

Dressed in her pyjama suit,
We all do say, 'You're cute!'

Each day she likes to play . . .

A Teletubbies lover,
A squeaky bunny mother,
Oh, I do love being her brother!

Ellis Harris-Boulter (11)

My Role Model

My favourite person
Let me tell you
But please read on
Because it's all true

She's funny
She's kind
She's everything to me
She cares for me
And looks after me

She is so fantastic
Only because she is enthusiastic

However, to me she is like a star
That shines in the night

My one
My favourite person
Is my mum.

Stacey Dalton (15)

My Nan

My favourite person is my nan,
She's kind and caring and always sharing,
Love and gifts and many things,
Nan is always happy and always sings.
When I talk to Nan, she understands
And makes me feel safe when I'm in her hands,
She laughs and jokes and joins in our fun,
She gets out the swimming pool in the sun.
My nan's so special and means so much,
She always seems to have that special touch,
That's why I love her so much.
I wanted to share and tell the rest,
That my nan is the best of the best!

Aimy-Lea Spence (11)

Without You

Without you I'm like
A pot with no gold
I'm like Shannon with no shoes
Or ice that's not cold

Without you I'm like
Santa with no sack
I'm like a teddy with no hair
Whenever you're gone, I want you back

Without you I'm like
Cereal with no milk
I'm like a jacket with no zip
Or a dress with no silk

Without you I'm like
A child with no toys
So together we make
Lots of *noise!*

Chloe Adamson (11)

Punchie And Me

Punchie is my dog
And he's my best friend.

He plays with me all day long,
Right up to the end.

He wags his tail and gives a bark,
When we play fetch in the park.

For a treat when we are home,
I give him a tasty bone.

But his favourite thing of all,
Is not his bone or his ball.

It's Lucas Courtney
And that's *me!*

Lucas Courtney (6)

My Best Friend Talia

It's love but it's friendship,
It's alone but we're together,
It's life changing but it's tender,
My friendship with Talia.

It's easy but it's complicated,
It's agreeable but it's arguable,
It's simple bit it's fun,
Hanging out with Talia.

It's amazing but it's normal,
It's out of this world but it's in it,
It's a dream but I'm doing it,
Laughing with Talia.

Now we are split up,
Our friendship could change,
Stronger or weaker,
With me and my best friend Talia.

Sarah Winkle (11)

Millie Rose

You are gorgeous, you are small
You make me feel ten feet tall!
Into this world last month you came
And you were given a lovely name
Your perfect face with turned-up nose
And soft, smooth skin and tiny toes
My life has changed so much since then
You are now my very best friend
As time goes by, we will grow up
Just like a dog with its pup
I'll leave school when you begin
I'll tell you what it's like, by then
But just now I'll give you peace
As you are my little darling niece.

Sunnygrace Darling (11)

My Favourite Person

Archie is my lovely dog,
He is a super buddy,
But when he's having fun outside,
He often gets quite muddy.

Archie or 'Arch' as I call him,
Has beautiful ginger fur,
He seems always to be happy,
If he was a cat, I bet he'd purr.

Archie is an amazing friend,
I tell him all my wishes,
He can tell when I'm sad or ill
And gives me bit wet kisses.

Archie can do fantastic tricks,
If we give him yummy treats,
He can do simple ones like 'sit' and 'wait'
And he waves to everyone he meets.

Molly Rose Mooney (11)

My Dog . . .

My dog is a nut,
She is the colour of soot.
She often snores
And has four paws.
She loves to play fetch
And is nice to sketch.
She loves to be stroked
And loves to be soaked.
She loves to chew sticks,
She's a Labrador mix!
She likes to swim in the sea
And to run free.
Sometimes she's naughty and cheeky and such,
But Martha, I love you, so very, very much!

Amelia Perring (10)

From London To Land's End

David and Adrienne lived in the flat above
From the day I was born, they sent their love.
When I moved with my parents far away
They never failed to come and stay.

David teaches history and at school he's feared
He's never to be seen without his beard!
He makes you laugh with all his jokes
Whether in sunshine, rain or smoke.

Adrienne is gentle, caring and kind
With a wonderfully creative, happy mind.
When I see her, she always brings a surprise
The red box and its contents amazed my eyes!

Jumping in waves, painting and drawing
Inventing a game, walking and talking.
Several times my age, but I don't care
The things I love, they eagerly share.

Naomi Johns (9)

My Dear Loving Father

When I'm feeling blue and my arms are wrapped around my chest,
You scoop me up, rock me and tell me I'm the best.
When I'm feeling pain and tears are trickling down my pale face,
You kiss me and act like I'm the winner of a million mile race.
When I feel angry and my fists are clenched, purple and blue,
You kneel down and look into my eyes like no other adult could do.
When my face is glowing and I'm beaming with pride,
You tell me the things I want to hear and treat me like a bride.
When my mouth is exploding with laugher and I can't contain my glee,
You smile broadly then hold my hand and join in with the giggling spree.
Now you've gone I miss you so and every day my heart aches,
I dream about you and cry before I awake.
There's so many things I want in my life out of them all I'd rather
Have you my dear, kind and loving father.

Debra Chown (12)

Super-Duper Mum

Mum likes candles
She likes growing flowers
Every second of the day she is busy
That's Super-Duper Mum!

Mum always makes me smile
She helps me with my homework
Every day she makes breakfast
If it wasn't for her, it wouldn't be the same!

Mum arranges birthday parties
She buys the best birthday cakes
Every year she makes it special
If it wasn't for her, it wouldn't be the same!

She's a very special mum
She's a very special person
She's not just Mum
She's Super-Duper Mum!

Chhandni Patel (9)

My Nan - My Favourite Person

My nan is my favourite person,
She is so cool,
She bakes for me and spoils me
And does loads of things for school.
She always sticks up for me,
Even when I'm bad,
She always makes me smile,
Even when I'm sad.
My nan would do anything for me,
She lets me sleep over
And even cooks my tea.
I love my nan, she is the best,
She doesn't even come near the rest,
Thank you Nan, for being my nan.

Jacob Ball (11)

My Favourite Person

My favourite person, of course, is me
But there are also my friends and my family
No, I think I'll change my mind
My favourite person is Sarah, so kind.

Sarah is my BFF
If we fall out, she's still the best
Her hair is golden, her eyes bluey-green
Her favourite thing is the TV screen.

She loves her sweets, some vegetables too
Her favourite colour is a light blue
Every day she comes out of school
She either says, 'Boring!' or, 'That was cool!'

So, you can see she is a great mate
Even if we have a debate
From now on, I hereby declare
She's my favourite person of love and care.

Hayley Alcorn (11)

She's All Mine!

I cry,
I laugh,
I smile,
I'm happy when she's around.
She's so special to me,
I cannot believe.
No, I can't.
But now I know,
When I'm sad I can run to her,
And she'll hold out her arms,
To give me a hug.
And when I laugh and when I smile,
She laughs with me and smiles as well.
I love you Mum, you're special to me!

Daina Hartley (10)

Ozzy - My Favourite Furry Friend

When I woke up on Christmas Day
I couldn't believe my eyes
The present Santa left for me
Was the very best surprise

A little fluffy kitten
He was cute and black and white
I called my kitten Ozzy
Cos that name, it just seemed right

Ozzy's always playful
Ozzy's really cool
Ozzy's pleased to see me
When I come home from school

Ozzy makes me happy
He never makes me sad
Ozzy's fun to have around
He's the best friend I ever had.

Mya Patience (7)

My Favourite Person - Grandad

Grandad taught me how to fish with a fishing net
Grandad was the kindest man you have ever met
Grandad picked me up from school nearly every day
Grandad helped look after me and take me out for days
Grandad taught me how to whistle, but not how to sing
Grandad told me stories about everything
Grandad let me read his story books when I stayed with him and Nan
Grandad made me laugh as he was a funny man
Grandad did silly things to entertain us
Grandad used to take us out on the bus
Grandad taught me all about birds, butterflies and trees
Grandad taught me to stay still near bumblebees
Grandad was the very best and I was sad he died
But I have my special memories of him, deep inside.

Cara McKeown (8)

My Mummy

My mum is ever so cool
And cares about me and my school
She is a person I adore
And is a person I will never abhor

What a wonderful mum she is
She is a person who I miss
My mum is sweet and kind
There is no other mum you can find

She is pretty, clever and smart
And absolutely loves books and art
Reading and writing is her speciality
And is always neat and natty

She is brighter than a shining star
And I miss her if she is near or far
My mum is the best
But sometimes I can be a pest.

Riddhima Gade (10)

Daddy Cool

He's a . . .
Super smirker,
Late time snorer,
Homework borer,
Every time . . .

Hobnob hogger,
21 mile jogger,
Cricket crazy,
A bit lazy,
All the time . . .

He's fashion sad,
So glad I have my . . .
Dad!

Jamal Kherry (10)

My Favourite Person

My favourite person is not
My mum, dad or gran,
Because he's not even human,
A woman or a man!

He only comes in winter,
When there is snow and ice,
He never has a temper,
He's kind and really nice.

He has a hat and scarf,
Two buttons for his eyes,
A carrot for his nose,
What a nice surprise!

Now maybe you have guessed
That I'm a really big fan
Of my favourite person
Frosty, the snowman!

Charlotte Revel (12)

Friendships Never End

Our friendship started when we met,
Now it will never end.
We are chatting to each other all the time,
We are totally the best of friends,
We share each other's secrets,
We share each other's lies.
Whatever the truth about us,
We're there when someone cries.
My best friend is older than me
But I don't really mind,
Whatever happens to me, she is really kind.
Me and her are best of friends
We will always be, until life ends.

Maxine Kassandra Velasco (10)

My Favourite Person

My favourite person is my grandpa,
He's always there for me,
I don't know what I'd do without him,
I'd feel incomplete, you see.

Every time I visit,
There's always lots to do,
Making scrapbooks, having fun
And going to the park too.

If I'm feeling down,
Or ill, sick or sad,
He will cheer me up with lots of jokes,
There are always laughs to be had.

He's the best grandpa ever,
So I would like to say,
Thank you for all your love and happiness,
It's really made my day!

Madeleine Brooks (12)

Down At The Lake With My Best Friend, Jake

I went to the lake,
With my best friend, Jake.
Jake had a headache,
I had a toothache.
So we went to sleep, which was a big mistake,
There was a snake down by the lake.
The snake bit us and gave us a shake,
Suddenly, we were awake.
I saw a *big* snake,
Which looked so fake.
Jake said, 'Give me a break!'

Rahsaan Corbin (9)

My Rabbit, Poppy

She may not be a person,
But I love her very much,
She is a little lop-eared bunny,
That happens to be Dutch.

I love my family too,
But she is the one,
That makes me smile and giggle,
When all the hope is gone.

She wakes me in the morning,
With a nibble at my toes,
I wonder what she's thinking . . .
Or is she just saying, 'Please, I want more toast!'?

I would like to close this poem,
By saying I love her so much . . .
That when we bought my Poppy,
We spoilt her with lots of treats and a mega-sized hutch!

Georgia Clarke (11)

My Cat, Marm

My cat, Marm, is so full of charm
He sits on my bed, just waiting to be fed.
When all is done, we'll have some fun,
We may just hop, jump, skip and run.

He's older now and sleeps a lot more,
But when the wind blows, he's out the back door.
He doesn't stay long, but he sits for a while
And on his face is a big, wide smile.

He sits on our telly and his tail hangs down,
He's white and orange and golden brown.
His eyes are closed, there's not a peep,
That's because, he's fast asleep!

Adam Simons (10)

My Granda

My granda is the very best,
The best that you could wish,
His jokes make me laugh out loud,
Cos they are funny-*ish!*

From finding beasties in the garden,
To making dens in the park,
We have always been really happy,
Or as 'happy as a lark'.

He calls me names, like 'Little Fella',
Or sometimes 'Bonny Lad',
He claims he's better at football than me,
But if so, it's by a tad!

But he's more than just a granda
And I just think it's great,
That he's a granda and a footballer,
But also my best mate!

Stephen Peter Burton (11)

My Favourite Person

My favourite person is Emily,
She is my best friend,
We always stick together,
And it will never ever end.

We've known each other since nursery,
Right the way through to Year 6,
She loves to go to the cinema,
And choose her pick 'n' mix.

We go to Coedylan Primary,
Our head teacher is Mr James,
We have a silver shed,
Which is packed with fun and games.

Megan Davies (10)

Hard To Choose

My favourite person
That's a bit tricky
The situation I'm in
Seems a bit sticky

Who do I choose?
Mum, Dad, brother or sister?
I love them all equally
This is a twister!

Friends and animals
People that care
A lot of love
For all to share

I have room in my heart of love
For more than a few
I even have a special place
Just for *you!*

Ellisha Gilbert (10)

Bandit The Cat

B eautiful creature
A mazing and trustworthy
N ever, ever sad
D aring and brave
I love him
T he beautiful cat, Bandit

T here forever
H igh leaper
E asy to love

C razy and caring
A nimal eater
T he beautiful cat, Bandit.

Tonita Holloway (9)

96

My Mum

Movie watcher
Dinner cooker
Keen talker
Good looker.

Homework helper
Generous carer
Hard worker
Flip-flop wearer.

Taxi driver
Football cheerer
Wine taster
Problem hearer.

Music listener
Chocolate lover
Book reader
Great mother!

Jordan Dunkley (10)

My Favourite Person - My Best Friend

There's this guy who's always there for me,
He's there for me when I'm sad.
Loads of times we've laughed with glee,
And when he takes my hand.

I know that I can trust him,
With my secrets dark and deep,
He's not the slightest small bit dim,
I dream about him when I sleep.

He's the best friend I've ever known,
He's not ever, ever greedy,
The seeds of our friendship have been sown,
His name is Marcus Seeney.

Grace Edwards (12)

97

Charlie, My Cat

I have lots of favourite people,
But this one was just great,
It was my fluffy cat,
Who was my favourite mate.

I was his favourite person, I think,
He was with me such a lot,
His favourite place was my bean bag,
Even from when I was just a tot.

Now I'll tell you one of his funny ways,
When we were about to eat,
He sat on a chair, expecting some food,
That would have been a very rare treat.

But now that he has died,
What a different life we have led,
He was such a fantastic pet,
But now Charlie, my cat, is dead.

Bethan Law (9)

My Favourite Person

My favourite person,
Is a very tough decision.
But if I had to make it,
I could not make it with precision.

I would pick my friend Polina,
Being confident and proud.
She's got a flexible body and
Is opposite to loud.

She is really friendly,
Loyal and kind.
So that's my favourite person –
It shall now be signed.

Madeline Ashman (10)

The Best Thing That Happened To Me

Fluffy is the best thing that has happened to me,
Having Fluffy as a pet is one of the great joys of my life,
It is very cool to interact with Fluffy, besides a human being,
Fluffy seems to be more funny than my friends,
Fluffy is the best thing that has ever happened to me,
He has a special ability to comfort me,
Somehow just being able to cuddle him,
Kiss him on the forehead,
Also look into his big, brown eyes,
Is enough to make me feel better after a rough day,
Fluffy is the best thing that has ever happened to me,
He is the lead to my pencil,
The button to my red jacket,
The love from my heart,
The colour to the rainbow,
If I didn't have Fluffy, I wouldn't know what I'd do,
Fluffy is the best thing that's ever happened to me!

Ameera Latif (12)

Ali's Cat

I have a cat with three legs,
He doesn't run, he hops instead,
He sleeps on my nan's bed.

He gets up to eat, then goes back to sleep,
Probably dreams about doing it again.

My other cat is called Fluffy,
I held him near,
I got up one morning
And he wasn't here,
I cried for a week,
I couldn't sleep.

At least I have my other cat,
Until fate gets him as well.

Alastair Smith (11)

My Favourite Person Is My Mum

My favourite person is my mum
She loves to make some tasty dishes
But when I go out to play
She always spots me and thinks I've gone missing
My mum has lovely hair
It's just like a black wooden chair
It's really nice to see if you were me
I would go out and smile with glee
But I always make my mum a hot pot of tea
Because my favourite person is my mummy
When you get to know her you could see
That she's an intelligent woman
You can see my mum loves me
I love her, because that is what mums do
Because they love you as much as anything
They would kiss you a goodnight sleep
'Cause that's my mum!

Pia Agarwal

My Favourite Person

My favourite person is my mum,
She is very kind,
She is the very best Mum, even though she is blind.

We are always up to something,
Does not matter what we do,
I love my mum more than the world and that is very true.

We are always going shopping,
Every single day,
If we are not sure about something, we'll buy it anyway.

She brought me up very well,
She's a brilliant mum, you can tell,
I appreciate everything you do,
The best mum in the world, it's true!

Lucy Stone (11)

My Best Friend, Emily

My favourite person is my best friend, Emily,
You and me forever,
Friendship will never end, as for us, we love to laugh and sing,
Vote for Emily, my best friend,
She is the best on rainy days.
I sit on the couch, look out the window waiting for Emily
                                                    to wave,
I let her in, climb under a blanket and turn it into a cave,
We talk about right, we talk about wrong, our rainy days are
                                                    never too long,
I eat in hers, she sleeps at mine, I wish she could stay over
                                                    all of the time.
People think we're sisters, Emily and I are just best friends,
Rough times, good times, then it's time to pretend . . .
Silly we are, naughty we're not, laughing all the time,
Oh what a friendship we've got . . .
So I hope you have a friend like I do . . . Emily my best friend.

Holly Davis (11)

My Daddy

He may be tall and have big feet,
Grey hair and love to eat.
Fixes things, moans and groans,
Always working hard and never off the phone.

Teaches me things every day,
Like how to cook and how to behave.
He makes me smile because that's his way,
Apart from that, he likes to have his say.

He's the household doctor when I'm feeling ill,
He makes me well, he's the magic pill.
But that's my dad, always on the ball,
He deserves a medal for being at my beck and call.

Abigail Storrie (12)

Mr Sled

My favourite person is someone you might know,
Someone who is special to me, someone who likes snow.
They're someone who is white,
Someone that's in sight,
When it comes to winter they're an absolute delight!

My favourite person is always having fun,
Always in the snow,
Playing with everyone,
Big black eyes,
Bright orange nose,
Three brown buttons,
And a striking pose!

My favourite person is called Mr Sled,
'Merry Christmas!' he shouted as the children fled,
He freezes near the Christmas lights, decorations and trees,
Can *you* guess who he might me?

Christina Petrou (10)

The Army

If the army did not fight for England,
In the First and Second World Wars,
There would be chaos everywhere
And I don't want that to happen at all.

They died for us,
They fought for us,
They killed for us,
They got injured for us.

Why do they do this for us?
What do we do for them?
Please Lord, help them fight,
And be strong for their families tonight.

Rebecca Hammond (11)

My Friend Bear Called Tatty Teddy

I've got a friend
And he loves the West End.

His name is Tatty Teddy
And he's got a rather big belly.

He's a big ball of fluff
And he's not that tough.

His blue nose is so cold
And he looks really old.

With fur that's grey,
He sits there every day.

He loves to travel,
Also likes eggs scramble.

Even though he doesn't speak,
He's still there without a squeak!

Chloe Collins (11)

My Grandad

My grandad is a man of many talents,
Making and doing,
Chopping and gluing,
Doing jobs better than my dad could do.

We'd have ice cream eating contests
And stories of Mum as a child,
Funny old sayings
And catchy little songs.

My grandad is an amazing man,
Whom I look forward to seeing,
(As well as Grandma's famous Sunday roasts),
But best of all,
He's my grandad
And I couldn't ask for more.

Olivia Dodson (11)

Caramel, My Guinea Pig

I love the times when we cuddle,
When you lie down on my lap and sleep.

I love the times that we talk,
Until we lose our voices.

I love it when you do a cute squeal of delight
When you see me.

I love the times that you pop corn,
When it is time for a run around.

I love the way you munch greedily on a treat I gave you,
After a good training session.

I love the times that I bathe you,
When your satin buff coat gleams like the sun.

You are my best friend, Caramel
And we have so much fun!

Anna Ross (9)

Stella

My best mate,
My one and only,
My best mate,
I'm never lonely.

Ever since primary,
Even when she moved,
It's been her all along,
We've always been a two.

Forever she shall stay,
The pair of us together,
She's my Alice,
I'm her Bella,
But really, she's my . . .
Stella!

Sophie Long (11)

104

Andy

We love to go on walks in lush green fields
And love to smell our dinner when teatime yields.

We always have a cuddle
And hate all puddles.

I like to play with him and teach him a trick,
He really is a softy and your feet he likes to lick.

My friend has long white hair and a little wet nose,
When he sniffs your feet, it tickles your toes.

I wouldn't say he's short, just quite small,
He can be really cheeky and burst my favourite ball!

He is quite naughty and can often be bad,
Let's just say he's barking mad!

My friend is my dog and I love him so,
I think he's really cute, don't tell him though!

Charlotte Harvey (10)

My Brother

My brother is fast,
White like lightning,
He will do anything to win the task.

Around the bend,
Rocketing to the end.

My brother is *mad!*
Face all red,
But he is still the best I've ever had.

My brother is always fun,
Yellow like a ball,
But runs away when there's work to be done.

My brother - *I love him!*
Well, most of the time!

Kieran Mulroy (10)

My Favourite Person!

My favourite person is my brother
He's much more fun than my mother,

Although he chooses not to speak
He's always, always full of cheek,

Today he made me wait a while
He likes to limit his great big smile,

He would never try to cause any trouble
He's really happy in his own wee bubble,

Although people look and frown
He never lets it get him down,

Autism is his obstacle in life
It brings with it a lot of strife,

So, as far as brothers go
He's the one I love to know.

Chloe Kennedy (11)

My Grandad

My grandad is skinny and weak,
Grey hair and stylish hat to look cool,
He drinks endless cups of tea.

But there is something strange about my grandad,
He wears colourful shirts, skin-tight jeans
And zooms me around in his amazing fast car,
He is a busy man with a job and has a diary to book me in.

He has got a very strange, but busy job,
He looks after kites,
He just sits over there all day long, drinking cups of tea,
Chatting with young children and selling kites.

My grandad has a place of honour,
Deep within my heart,
He has been my superhero,
Right from the very start.

Munish Chopra (10)

My Sister, My BFFL

My favourite person is my sister,
She makes me smile when the day goes by
And when I am down, she makes everything alright.

She's always there when you need some advice,
I'll admit I am not that good at all times.

She eats lots of chips, day and night,
But we never fight on a single bite.

Sometimes I forget she is my sister,
We are best friends.

We always share our ups and downs in our life,
She always says she never heard a single word.

That's the relationship between me and her,
She's not only my sister, she's my BFFL -
Best friend for life.

Noor-Ul Sabah (13)

Meeeeeeeee!

My favourite person is myself
I love me and not the elf
I'm a devil, I'm not sweet
That's the truth, I'm not a treat
I'm the best, I'm to be
What your eyes cannot see
Me, me, me!

Saffron Roberts (11)

Jessica

My best friend is Jessica, she is very kind to me,
in the summer we'd dance and play and go swimming for free.

One night she came for a sleepover, and had smoked sausage for tea,
we had a big pillow fight and laughed and laughed with glee.

When we went swimming, the treasure island was out,
we jumped in the deep end and played and played about.

Our friendship is special, it's very close to us,
if we stop playing, we might cause a fuss.

We both love each other, we are like two peas in a pod,
but sometimes Jessy, could be a bit odd.

Now the poem's done,
I've had a lot of fun,
thank you for reading,
and well done for succeeding!

Carly Peters (9)

My Granny - A Poem For My Great-Grandmother Aged 85

Me and my granny are best friends,
We're both strong and brave.
She keeps me going when time is rough,
That's the thing that she has got.
We go on all sorts of adventures,
Like sailing on the Titanic.
But when that stops, she helps me a lot,
So to make you proud, Granny
I will always love you!

Granny, you're always there even if you're not,
I will always feel you right in the middle of my heart,
So I write this in all the things we do,
So here is a massive, *thank you!*

Eleanor Christon (10)

My Favourite Person

My favourite person is no human,
It's Baxter.
Eyes sparkling, coat shining, ears gleaming,
In the dictionary he is under *gorgeous, handsome* and *beautiful.*
He's faster than me, because has four legs,
Each leg was a gorgeous brown.
He wagged his tail when he was happy,
Every day he was happy, so he always wagged his tail.
Cats and dogs were his friends,
Because he never even chased a single cat!
'Baxter,' we said, 'Sit!' So he did, 'Good boy!'
Then we gave him a treat.
Woofs, smiles and laughs, happiness,
His life was full of happiness.
My favourite person is no human,
He is an angel in Heaven.

Annabel Cammish (10)

My Best Friends

Y assmine is caring and loving
A lways there for me
S weet and sensitive
S trong and cares for me
M akes you feel like family
I ndependent and free
N o one hates her
E njoying her time at Highbury Fields, while I'm at Acland Burley

J ensila helps me when I'm down
E njoying her life
N othing can knock her down
S till thanking her for the best nine years of her life
I ntelligent and older than them all
L oving and helpful
A lways been there, but now she's gone to EGA.

Salmeh Shangama (11)

My Sister, Kitty

My sister, Kitty
Is very pretty
Her hair's like silk
And she laps up milk.
She has a pink nose
And scratchy toes
Her eyes, so bright
Can see at night.
She pads down the corridor
And through my door
She jumps on my bed
And sleeps by my head.
She Curls in a ball
So *very* small
And purrs away
Until night is day.

Edwin Scott (9)

The Best Nan In The World

My nan is always with me everywhere I go
She tells me all the things I really need to know
If I fall over, cut or bruise my knee
She will always take tender care of me
She will always listen to everything I say
Sometimes she will let me come and stay
Whenever I go to tea, I always smell the air
She will always take a lot of care
Watching TV in the afternoon is not her thing
So she'd rather be out in the open air in the hot spring
My nan would rather clean than sit around
I think she should be crowned
My nan is the best nan in the world as you can see
My poem is about my nan,
She is the best, I hope you agree.

Katie Way (9)

Smokey And Smudge

Smokey and Smudge are my pet rats,
White and grey and black and white,
Their tails are long and smooth,
Cute little faces and tiny little noses,
Their fur is soft like a feather,
Little teeth, they never bite,
Black shiny eyes and long whiskers,
Crawling through tubes,
Climbing over boxes
And poking their noses out of the holes,
Running up my sleeve,
Hiding in my jumper,
Sitting on my shoulder
And crawling along my legs,
I love my pet rats,
When you see them, I hope you love them too.

Asha Jade Bott (5)

I Love My Mummy

I love my mummy
She loves me too
We play games together
And we go swimming too
We walk the dogs called Meg and Jake
I ride my bike which I love to take
We meet other dogs who growl and bark
As we are walking through the park
Then it's time to go home for tea
And I've been as busy as a bee
After tea, Mummy says, 'Time for bed'
And I lay down my tired head
To dream of what I've done today
And think of tomorrow as another day
And hope it is sunny so we can play.

Faith Bryant (6)

Joshua And Rhys

Joshua and Rhys
We are friends together
Joshua and Rhys
We all have each other
Joshua and Rhys
We all do things together
Joshua and Rhys
We play together like building dens and tree houses
When I am sad
They make me happy
When I am worried
They make me feel safe
When we are together
They makes me feel strong
Joshua and Rhys
We are friends forever!

James Stevens (8)

My Great Grandad

Although we have never met
there are things I will not forget
pictures hanging from the walls
my favourite of them all
the one that made Great Nan your wife
and the one of you in uniform
ready to fight in World War II
you were so brave and courageous
even when you became a prisoner of war
I feel so lucky to be part of your family
I feel you watching over me
and guiding me on my path
I hope I am as lucky to be as brave as you
and my love for you will never ever pass
I love you Great Grandad x

Jenson Nicholls (8)

Who Is My Favourite Person?

It is hard to decide who my favourite person is,
Family, friends or celebrities.
There are so many people whom I admire,
To be like them is what I desire.
My family gives me comfort whenever I'm sad,
After talking to them I always feel glad.
My kind friends help me in school,
If I'm lost or stuck or feeling uncool!
My pet guinea pigs bring me joy,
Whenever I feel 'oh boy'!
I've got loads of homework to do,
If I don't do it all I'll get a detention or two.
I enjoy reading up on the celebrities I know,
And I sometimes watch them on a TV show.
But in the end oh how happy I can be,
When I am with my family.

David Bissell (12)

My Imaginary Friend

My imaginary friend
Is there for me
When my mum goes away.

My imaginary friend
Plays with me
When my mum goes away.

My imaginary friend
Tells me stories
When my mum goes away.

My imaginary friend
Can eat ice cream for breakfast
Only when my mum goes away!

How is your imaginary friend?

Claudia Shaw (10)

McFly

How they rock out like sand
Brains and brawn to create music.
Fun and excitement.
Fans scream as loud as they can,
as they take the stage,
once they start it is amazing.
The one I like is Harry,
he brings a tear to my eye,
with the love for McFly it is unbelievable.
For when they leave the stage,
the fans they scream as loud as they can,
a job well done for the four boys,
I'd love to see them live,
and have a back stage pass,
as they travel worldwide.
They are the youngest band in the world.

Caley Wylie (10)

My Favourite Furry Friend

My favourite person is my pet dog Sox.
We play together, go walkies and I throw him sticks.
Then he looks at me with his beautiful green eyes,
As if he wants to tell me something.
I wish I knew what it was,
When I get in he races up and down the hall,
his tail wagging playfully.
I laugh at him when he chases his tail.
Then in the garden I throw his ball to him.
Barking like crazy he jumps up and down at me.
As I do my homework he curls up and the end of my bed.
I take him for a walk,
both of us loving every moment of it.
I love Sox! I really do.

Chelsea Gosling (11)

Colin

My favourite person 2009
Is my grandad, he's all mine
I bake cakes with him and mess around
He's always acting like a silly clown
We blow up balloons and set them free
And sometimes he plays tennis with me
He's great and he's so much fun
I love him to bits he's number one
He plays the guitar
He's great at it, I sing with him but I ruin it
But he doesn't mind cos he loves me lots
Then he just says I am at the top of the pops
Me and my grandad are like best friends
I wish I could be with him until the end
It's always sad to say goodbye
But I know tomorrow I'll be saying, 'Hi!'

Amber Kelsi Brant (10)

My Grandpa

My grandpa is so very special
I love him more and more
we spend a lot of time together
but I wish we could spend some more
I help him with his puzzles
because they are hard to do
and if I didn't help him
I don't know what he would do
he is always in the garden
pulling out the weeds
I often go and talk to him
to find out what he needs
he looks after my nanny so very well
and I think it is time to tell
how very special he is to me
and will always be.

Chelsea Newman (9)

My Mum

She cleans, cooks and works hard for us all,
She'll do a job if it's big or small,
She'll cheer us up when we're glum,
Yes, you guessed it, it's my mum.

Not many people are like my mum,
She cooks our meals that are yum,
She dashes around like someone who's mad
And sorts us out when we've been bad.

How many people, do you think,
Would want a mum like mine in a blink?
Who hugs them, cares for them and loves them dearly
And is just like Dad, well, nearly!

Emily James (11)

My Favourite Person

My favourite person is dark and slim
And rather dim,
With flat black hair,
I wish I could wear,
He has a small, black shirt
And his name is Bert,
You cannot see him,
'Cause no one can please him,
Except for me,
I hope to go down in history,
When he eats a tart,
He is bound to fart,
But now I must go,
I have a show,
I'm not going round the bend,
He's my imaginary friend!

Bryher Semonin (9)

Jade

She will always be my bestest friend
She will always be there for me
We may have our ups and downs
But she will be there for me

She's funny, she's kind and totally amazing
I will always be there for her
She's lovely to be with, she's such a star
I will always be there for her

She's fashionable, smart, totally cool
She's ever so special to me
We play together, she has wonderful ideas
She's ever so special to me.

Caitlyn Ephgrave (11)

My Favourite Person - JK Rowling

She writes and she writes and she writes
Of witches in black and purple tights
She tells of all sorts of creatures prowling
This wonderful author is JK Rowling!
Most of her stories are full of magic
The Harry Potter series was a mythical classic
How her stories amaze me
Full of suspense and fantasy
Some of her tales, spooky and scary
With monsters all big and hairy!
How does Harry manage to stay alive?
With all those deadly monsters, it's impossible to survive!
It feels like her stories are speaking to me
Open one of her books and I'm sure you'll see!
Reading her books, whilst my heart beats faster
Hypnotising me, as though she were my master!

Natasha Pavey (10)

My Mum

My favourite person is my mum
To me she's like my closest chum
She always has advice for me
And also cooks a yummy tea!

Whenever I am feeling down
She picks me up from off the ground
And should I ever need her help
She's there before I even yelp!

I think that you can all now see
Just why my mum's so special to me
I love her to the moon and back
And I'm sure she already knows that!

Charlotte Jones (11)

My Favourite Person

My favourite person is bouncy and cool,
She's fun on outings and strict with school,
My favourite person, she's that and all,
She's got green eyes and is pretty tall.

She is a shining star in society,
Her heart is full of love and pity,
She is the sun that enlightens my day
She never lets my hopes fade away.

She's my course of conduct,
My path,
My object of such affection,
My love,
My strong supporter of a cause,
My pillar,
My mum.

Yousra Benrahal (12)

My Brother

I really like my brother
He's just like my mother

My brother loves to play football
And he's very tall

My brother is very funny
He wastes his money on honey

My brother loves his cat
Who is very fat

My brother likes to run
And he's very fun

My brother thinks he's cool
He loves to jump in the swimming pool

And that's my brother!

Anam Akhtar (10)

Mum

Loving you is the best thing on Earth
The way you smile at me with your beautiful smile
The way you laugh on the phone
And make me laugh with you
The way you take me shopping
And let me buy the coolest things
I love you every day in every way
You are so special to me
I'm glad you're my mum
I love you
I love you
I love you!

Niamh Fahey (11)

My Favourite Person

This is a poem for my friend, Charlotte
She is friendly, nice and polite to me
We play on the playground and in the park too
Then we go home and stop and have tea
We get ready for bed before eight o'clock
Because having a sleepover is good fun too
We are excited and happy, waiting for midnight to strike
Trying to stay awake is really hard for us to do
We wake in the morning, hearing the birds singing
Really tired from our lack of sleep
We'd talked and laughed until the early hours
Now we have a lovely memory for us to keep.

Chloe Davidson (8)

Miley Cyrus

Although I have not met her, I'm sure she is kind,
She's pretty, happy, funny and everything I don't mind,
She's on my favourite TV show
And can sing really low,
One day I hope to meet her and have fun all the time,
But until that happens, I've got to wait and it's getting late,
I hope to be on her TV show, but when will that happen?
Will I ever see her? It is bound to happen,
I can't wait to have adventures in Hollywood,
Hope I don't fall in the mud!
But all I wanted to say, was that Miley Cyrus
In my heart, will always be my favourite.

Courtney Hillman (11)

My Favourite Person

He plays for LFC
His name is Stevie G
He celebrates his birthday
On the 30th of May
In the darkness, in the light
Without a doubt, he will fight
Liverpool will have the glory
They will be the headline story
He plays as number eight
I think he's truly great
I don't know about you
But he's the one I look up to!

Katie May Steele (10)

The End

My best friend is Sarah,
The end.
Wait! I forgot to say I can never scare her,
The end.
Hang on! I forgot to say she is a darer,
The end.
No, not really, I forgot some information,
I'll tell you it without hesitation . . .
She is . . . *um* . . .
Never mind!
The end.
Wait . . . !

Eleanor May (9)

A Friend Is My Favourite Person

She stands by my side through and through,
This is how I know it's true,
Never does she complain about my crazy ideas,
Even though she may have fears,
We make up when we fight,
Have a hug, ever so tight,
Each Christmas we sing with joy
And give each other a brand new toy,
On summer days lie in the light,
Have a sleepover and giggle all night,
She is my friend through and through
I am certain that is true!

Stefanie Octon (11)

My Super Dad

My dad is great,
My dad is funny,
My dad is like a superstar,
My dad rocks the house,
My dad helps with my homework,
My dad plays games
And has fun with me,
My dad is strong,
The best in the world,
If I cry, he will sort it out,
So I don't have to worry,
His hugs will cure it.

Conor Carr (10)

My Mum

My mum is the best,
She is always there for me,
Much like a humble bumblebee,
My first step, she was there to watch me,
Likewise when I watch her drink cups of tea.
My mum is kind,
If I do something wrong, she won't mind,
She always has a smile on her face,
Especially when I am running a race.
My dad's one in a million,
But my mum's one in a trillion,
My mum's the best!

Madeline Ivy Sirot-Smith (11)

My Favourite Person

My favourite person is the best I know
He warms my heart like a red, fiery glow
Whenever I am sad, I see him smile
That makes me laugh and giggle for a while
He runs around the house
Like a little mouse
He treats me so gentle and sweet
It makes me want to give him a golden treat
He pulls my hair and gives me a kiss
At night, his giggles I miss
My little bro is the best
He's my favourite person from the rest.

Samina Akhtar (8)

My Furry Friend

A big ball of fluff,
His fur is like the night sky.
Friendly, yet shy,
Heard, but not seen.
Loves a good fuss
And a bowl of ham.
Amazing at hunting,
Done in a flash.
Moonlit eyes
And ears always listening.
What more can I ask
From my furry little friend?

Leely Parsons-Davies (10)

Simply The Best Mum

My mum is the best
She's better than the rest
If she were a diamond, I'd pick her
She loves and cares
If I had to choose a mum, she'd be the one
She's so much fun
I couldn't simply live without my mum
Oh, I forgot to say, she's good at sums
She's a dream mother
She loves me and my brother
Nothing can replace her
'Cause I'll always love her.

Rumbidzai Dhewa (9)

My Sister - My Favourite Person

Sisters, what funny things they are
Some are vile and vicious
And some are kind and caring
My sister can be sweet as well as annoying
But . . .
There are some things . . .
I love most about my sister!
They are . . .
She helps me find my way
She shows me what is right and wrong
And she understands me!
That's what is so *special* about my sister, *Emma!*

Hannah Dove (11)

My Grandad

My grandad would sit me on his knee
And teach me all about history,
He would give me cuddles all day long
And sing me a silly song,
He'd take me to the caravan and push me on the swing,
He would walk me on the moors, till my feet were killing me,
He'd tell me stories he'd made up,
To make me laugh and cheer me up,
He'd read me books for hours on end
And when he died I thought my world would end,
This is for you, Grandad, I miss you no end,
You'll always be my favourite person.

Maisie Drewry (10)

Four In One

My favourite person is four in one,
it is made of loving, like a mum,
caring, like a dad,
observing, like a sister,
and kind, like a friend,
I have got all these people,
and so they make me happy,
from their attitude it passes to me,
for I *have* four in one.
My favourite people are all of these,
I keep them in a pile in my heart,
and I will never let them part.

Erica Marin-Lladós (11)

My Favourite Person - My Little Brother, Jack

My little brother, Jack, he is brand new,
He arrived in our family, out of the blue.
What a smile! What a cry!
Jack really is quite a guy.
He's started crawling and soon he'll walk,
I wonder what he'd say if he could talk?
Friday the 13th is unlucky, some may say,
But in our family, it was such a great day.
I'll watch out for him as much as I can,
I'm sure he'll grow to be a fine man!

Chelsy Donnelly (10)

My Sister

Lauren is so cool, she rocks the school
I love her because she gives lots of hugs
Lauren is the best in every quest
Sister, oh sister, I love you

Lauren is so great and she has lots of mates
We love to play around, she often plays the clown
Lauren is my number one, she's as bright as the sun
Sister, oh sister, I love you

I am her favourite sister, when she goes out, I miss her
We argue sometimes, but that does not change my mind
Sister, oh sister, I love you.

Isabel Hopley (7)

127

My Favourite Person

My grandpa, Hugh, was one in a few,
He gave me hugs and kisses when I was feeling blue,
His stories of old Scotland were funny, but true,
I'm glad I knew him, my grandpa, Hugh.

He visited us often with Gran,
I hope he knew I was such a fan,
I remember his laugh and his whistling too,
I am glad I knew him, my grandpa, Hugh.

I love him and miss him, but remember him often,
He was one in a million,
Grandpa Hugh, my favourite person.

Emma Wileman (10)

My Favourite Person

My favourite person is my big sister, Georgina,
She really makes me laugh and giggle,
Whenever I am in trouble, she is always there to help me
And we have so much fun together.
At school, she comes to see me every playtime,
To make sure I am OK,
Georgina is a great, fun person
And is smiling every day.

She might be older than me,
But she always believes in me!

So, that's my favourite person!

Jamie Griffin (6)

M U M

My mum just ain't a mum, she is a M U M:

M agical
U nderstanding
M other

To see my mum is like a gift I should never break,
The smell of her makes me feel like every day is as sweet as her,
When I hear her call my name, it is like I've been blessed,
If my mum tasted like anything, she would taste like chocolate
For she is soft, rich and heavenly,
My mum is the best person in the world
And nobody could change this!

Caliyah Jones (12)

My Pet Snails

M y pet snails
Y ellow, brown and grey

P lough along
E ating everything on their way
T ogether they lay 500 eggs in a day

S limy creatures, with
N ot unlike alien features
A lways leaving shiny trails
I
L ove
S nails!

Niko Kristic (9)

Top Teacher

My favourite teacher is truly the best,
He completely stands out from the rest!

I know he'll never strop about,
I can tell you this without a doubt!

I look forward when going to school,
Because I know he's really cool!

He'd help me when I'm sad,
He would say to me, 'Cheer up, lad!'

He's smart, friendly and fun,
That's why I vote him number one!

Pavan Indrayan (11)

My Rabbits

We were in Portugal and the wind was a-blowy
And all I could think of was Charlie and Snowy.

I was on my holiday and I got into habits
When all I could think of was my lovely rabbits.

I miss their smile and the feel of their fur
I really do miss Charlie and her.

I love my rabbits, I keep them within my clutch
Then I put them back in their hutch.

I think of them more and more
When I think of them resting in their straw.

Megan Nash (10)

Daniel Golec

D aniel is my baby cousin
A nd he is cute and so funny
N ever perfect
I t's so good to have him
E xcited blue eyes
L ittle man, full of mischief

G et ready
O h, here he comes
L oud as ever
E verybody's favourite boy
C uteness at maximum.

Alice Ghoda (8)

My Favourite Person Poem

My nan, she's always so sweet and kind,
When I go round there she kisses me, what a surprise,
She always has things to do, if it's dominoes, Scrabble and Monopoly too.
She has a buffet for dinner: ham, cheese, so much more that she prepares.
Then after dinner we play in the garden, so much fun
Then my nan makes ice cream, delicious,
Then we go in and the adults have a cup of tea
We watch a bit of telly and when it gets late we get ready to go.
Then she gives me, my brother and my sister £5 each,
We get in the car and wave, while we leave.
She does all this at 83!

Evangeline Trayhorn (11)

My Mum

A house worker,
A toy shopper,
A book reader,
A bath runner,
A child lover,
A food cooker,
A flower planter,
A cat feeder,
A vet traveller,
She's so much fun,
'Cos she's my mum!

Felix Loewenthal (8)

My Favourite Person

Cooks my meals, cleans my house,
Works all day, nine till three, pays the bills,
Drives the car, is my taxi,
Keeps me organised, gives me pocket money,
Washes my clothes, gives me love
And hugs me when I'm ill
And still loves me with all her heart
And her name begins with a C,
But it's not Cam, it's Catherine,
But I call her . . .
Mam!

Chloe Davies (13)

My Baby Brother

One like no other
People say he's just lazy
But I think he's just crazy
He is always sweet round his mother
But alone with me, he's no lover
Every time I do change his nappy
Always I smell something unhappy
Some people say he's really cute
While wearing his brand new black suit
Even though he's one like no other
He'll always be my baby brother!

Rajun Gill (10)

Mr Bell

Mr Bell is funny,
Mr Bell is smart,
I like him lots
And he's really good at art.

He teaches maths,
Science too,
He even told me
Who invented the loo!

He really likes history,
Especially England's victory!

Nicole Olivia Dallison (10)

My Favourite Person

I love my daddy
My daddy loves me
He spends a lot of time with me.

We go fishing
But he hooks a duck
And we do puzzles and read some books.

We like a cuddle
As we watch TV
But when it's bedtime
He says goodnight to me.

Tasmin Ellis (9)

My Baby Sis

My favourite person is my new baby sis
She's the one I love to kiss
She smells so good like bubbles and baths
And when she's older I'll help her with maths!

She giggles and smiles when she is all happy
But frowns and moans when she needs a new nappy
When she's older we'll go to the park
I'll cuddle her tight when she's scared of the dark

I'm so proud to tell you this
I love wee Zara, my new baby sis!

Zoe McKeown (10)

My Favourite Person

My best friend for life, who is very precious,
He gives me magnificent thoughts, which taste delicious,
The person who comes beside me in the pitch-black night if I get threatened
                                        with nightmares,
To see the lovely carved face he has in the earliest morning,
                                    that is very special,
The bond between him and myself is as strong as metal,
The joy and fascinating times of fun I have with him,
Of course, you should have guessed who he is,
It is my little brother indeed.

Brendon Rodrigo (10)

Marvellous Mum

My favourite person is very kind,
I just can't get her off my mind,
She never gets to rest,
It's my mum, she is the best,
We always sit down on the rugs,
While my mum gives me nice warm hugs,
Mum loves me very much,
She has a special touch,
My mum kisses me goodnight,
Then says, 'Sleep tight!'

Tilly Docherty (9)

My Grandma

My grandma was the best one ever,
She was wise and helpful, bright and clever.
Her apple pies were indescribable, the best without a doubt,
For all her functions she baked for, you could always pick hers out.
Everyone could talk to her, advice she would always give,
Her standards and morals incomparable on how your life to live.
Our dog, Midge, loved her immediately on sight,
He must have thought, *I'm coming home with you, this feels just right!*
She was very kind and considerate and always able to sort out my muddles
I miss my grandma!

David McKone (10)

My Favourite Person

He is Superman
He is a super banana
He is super clever
He is super crazy
He is super snappy
He is super happy
He is a super cook
He has a super look
My favourite person is
My granddaddy!

Erin Macuga (11)

Jackson!

You are special,
So much to learn and wonder about,
Your head spins like planets.
As you wave your hands like the queen,
Shooting up and crashing down,
Your eyes are shooting stars,
Darting round,
Never stopping,
You are a galaxy,
Miniature version!

Finn Manders (9)

Dad

Dad, they will always try to make you red in the face,
They will do the best possible in your life.
Without my dad, I would just burst into sadness
Whenever he buys me things, it always makes me feel loved and cared.
Whenever I think about my dad, he always makes me feel special inside
My bond between my dad and I, will always be strong,
Today, tomorrow and always.
Love your dad and cherish each moment you share together
You never know when those special moments
Can be taken away from you.

Rajandeep Daman (11)

My True Friend

Harley Barley is my true friend,
He's honey and white from top to end,
He looks like a teddy bear, soft and fluffy,
I give him cuddles, because he's my special puppy,
His eyes are gentle and brown,
He likes to do a Michael Jackson sound,
He makes me laugh when I'm feeling down,
He's really fun to have around,
Sometimes I think he's got his own doggy trend,
I am very fortunate to have such a loving friend.

Chenise Long (10)

My Brother

My brother is called Jack
And he likes to sit on my lap.
My brother is very sweet
And he rocks to his own beat.
My brother has blue eyes
And he likes to eat pies.
My brother likes school,
But some people say school isn't cool.
My brother is called Jack
And he likes to sit on my lap.

Hanna Swinburne (10)

My Favourite Person

Michael Jackson's killer beat,
Went down a big, massive treat.
Dancing zombies, killer steps,
Leaping through the graveyard sets.
Michael in the spotlight,
Will keep you jigging all through the night.
Although he died in 2009,
He's the greatest pop artist of his time.
That is why Michael is the best,
He will put you to the test.

Thabiti Rishi Aubeeluck Beckles (11)

My Friend

My friend is always with me and she fills me up with glee,
We have our ups and down, but I bribe her with some pounds.
There is something about us that gets me in a fuss,
Even though she looks like a clown, it doesn't make me frown.
She has a big, black cat,
But I just have a rat!
She plays with her cat and I play with my rat,
She has a portable fan, but I don't give a damn.
So, as you can see, she is a great friend,
Maybe I should give you her to lend!

Shreeya Parekh (10)

My Dad

My favourite person is my dad,
He comforts me when I'm sad.
If I feel like burying my head in the sand,
He's always there to hold my hand.
My dad is the bees' knees,
His favourite food is stinky cheese!
My dad is really daft,
He makes me laugh and laugh and laugh.
Dad makes me happy in lots of ways,
He leaves me smiling for many days.

Benedict Shackleford (10)

She's Called Dave

Dave, Dave,
With a heart like a wave,
She comes and she goes,
Hard to understand.
She does seem rather keen,
Even though she never knows the school routine.
Always wanted to make a band,
And one day she will compose.
But I will expose . . .
Her real name is Geraldine!

Jessica Li (13)

My Mum

Her smile is the brightest
Her hug is the tightest
I feel safe on her knee
And she just loves me
She sometimes shouts
'Eva, what's this all about?'
But when I say I'm sorry
She tells me not to worry
She's my number one
She's my mum.

Eva McCallion (7)

Ashley Young

You make me smile when I see you play
I just wish that I could meet you one day
We could play football together and laugh all day long
And maybe, just maybe, we could sing a few songs
Villa's Stadium is big, I've been there before
And you were the one who got the first score
I look up to you every time you play
And this is the message I'm trying to say
You are a great footballer and I just know
So go and thrash that football match, go, go, go!

Paige Winders (11)

My Kitten

My favourite person is my kitten,
Even though I have been bitten.
Sometimes she's a bit rough,
But she's usually full of love.
She hops around like a bunny,
With her tail up, which is very funny.
She'll jump up to catch a fly,
And soar around really high.
She's got black and white fur,
So now I know I'll never forget her.

Eva Ernstzen (10)

My Favourite Snowman In The Wind

My best friend is Snowy the snowman,
Who melted one winter day –
The wind called his name,
I remember when he was first made –
Roll, roll
Stack, stack
Buttons, buttons
Stick, stick
Carrot
A top hat and around him a warm scarf!

Dominique Camilleri (10)

My Dad

I love my dad, he is cool
He sometimes picks me up from school
He drives a big, silver van all over the place
In a hurry, no time to waste
He plays football for Red Star
They are the best we know by far
When they lose, he is cross
That's because he's the boss
So that's why I love my dad, 'cause he's the best
'Cause he is better than all the rest!

Lucy Robinson (6)

Wee Lizzy

I've known wee Lizzy since I was tiny
I wasn't at all whiney
Whenever she looks at me I smile because I know she is always there for me
As well as kind, she's mighty strong though she wouldn't hurt a fly
Lizzy's the greatest person I won't lie
Another thing she is very enthusiastic
Her cooking's fantastic
When I take a sip of her delicious soup, I say, 'Mmm, yummy!'
I've known wee Lizzy since I was tiny
Yep, you've guessed it, wee Lizzy is my mummy.

Isla Cole (10)

My Mum

My mum is always there for me
Standing at my side
There are many mothers out there
But no one as good as mine
She always makes me laugh and smile
When I'm feeling blue
If I ever have a problem
Mum's the one to turn to
She loves and cares for me with all her heart
That's her motherly party.

Michaela Cardone-Randall (12)

My Wonderful Grandma

My grandma is smaller than me,
She has a big loving heart made of gold.
My grandma, who is very special,
Always makes me feel special in some sort of way.

I love it that she never treats me any different from the others,
And that she never leaves any of us out.

I think she is an angel of the stars above,
And that is what makes her special to me!

Lauren Bott (12)

David Tennant

I think David Tennant is a great man,
I love his acting too.
I am one of his bestest fans,
I like to watch Doctor Who.

I think he is a very nice man,
I think he looks so cute.
I want his autograph,
But I'll have to wait at the end of the long queue!

Charlotte Murray (10)

My Favourite Person

I have a little brother who is small
Next to him I am very tall
His name is Jack and he's three
He always copies me, even my tea
He's very funny and follows me about
Sometimes it's too much and I shout
But I'd never be without my little bro
As I love him very much, right down to his toe!

Tommy Lush (10)

My Mum

My favourite person is my mum
Together we have so much fun
We sing and dance and skate and run
And on holiday, we play in the sun

My mum is pretty, funny and kind
If I am cross, she doesn't mind
She helps me with homework, because she is smart
And I love her with all my heart.

Sophie Kernachan (8)

My Favourite Person

My favourite person is my mum
Together we have lots of fun
We like to play games all day
And listen to what each other say.

We're on adventures all the time
Drinking lots of lemon and lime
We try to watch out for each other
'Cause I know that she's my mother.

Bracken Symonds (11)

Mum And Dad

My favourite person is my mum,
She used to have a great fat tum,
But now she's gone on a diet,
She always is all thin and quiet!
My other favourite person is my dad,
He's never, ever sad,
When he was a boy, he was bad
And now he is my dad!

Hannah Andrews (8)

I Love Cheryl Cole

Cheryl Cole from Girls Aloud,
Likes to entertain the crowd,
She's married to a football star,
Who likes to drive a nice big car,
She loves to dance, she loves to sing,
The X Factor is her thing,
She's a Geordie lass through and through,
But she likes to be with the crew.

Lauren Goldsborough (10)

Izzy

I know this may sound silly,
but my favourite person in the house is Izzy,
She likes to eat and thinks she rules the streets,
and perhaps she will one day.
She once killed a robin and did a bit of bobbin'
and starred in a movie called 'Shrek'
but the only reason I love her is
because she loves me whatever I say.

Amber Amor (11)

My Best Friend - Rebecca

R ebecca is reliable
E nthusiastic in lessons
B est of friends
E nergetic and full of fun
C lever and considerate
C aring and kind
A lways happy
   We will always be best friends!

Cary Hobbs (8)

Tribute

It's sad, but true
That a star I knew
Could have a life so tragic
His performances were magic
His moves and music will live on
Even though he's gone
A legend
Michael Jackson - King of Pop!

Paige Brookes (11)

Girls Aloud Kimberly

K ind soul
I ncredible voice
M agical hair
B eautiful eyes
E ntertaining smile
R adiant skin
L ucious lips
Y ou know she's my favourite.

Sophie Long (9)

My Wonderful Gran

My gran is a great cook
She has a very big recipe book.
My gran is not scary,
She's just like Little Mary.
I love her more than myself
And hope she always has good health.
I love Gran to little parts
I will always keep her in my heart.

Tiffany Lee (11)

Olly

Olly is a wally
He's always very jolly
He's my friend, my chum, my mate
He can get himself into a big state
Olly's very funny
He's like a big Easter bunny
Olly is a wally
My friend, my chum, my mate.

Jeorgia Carr (9)

My Fabulous Mum!

My mum is skilful, crazy and funny,
Her eyes sparkle like diamonds
And her voice is as sweet as a robin's tweet.
My fabulous mum is loving, caring and generous,
She helps me with my work,
She makes my yummy, scrummy tea,
But I love her the most, because she loves me.

Connor Woolley (10)

My Angel-Like Sister

She was pink, she was white, we were not alike,
She was cool, she was fine and at the time she was nine,
She was pretty, she was funny, she was just like a jar of soft, tasty honey,
She was my sister, she is my sister and I really, really miss her,
She's not here, she's not there, she's not anywhere,
But I know she's in Heaven, my lovely beautiful, adorable sister,
Monisa Gulfreen Qazi.

Momina Wafa Qazi (16)

I Love My Mum

My mum is the best,
Better than all the rest,
She's there for me to lie on,
A shoulder for me to cry on,
She's a very good cook,
Without a book,
That's why I love my mum.

Bethany Mellor (11)

My Mum

My mum is lovely and caring
She is always there for me
When I get home from school
She cooks me a tasty tea.
She is beautiful, loving and helpful
And when I feel unhappy,
Her warm cuddles make me happy.

Alexander Lee (8)

Daisy

My cat, Daisy, is a little crazy
She is never lazy
She likes to catch the birds so she has to wear a collar
She is worth a million dollars
She's cute, sweet, very unique
She likes to play outside and likes to hide
Then she comes inside and snuggles by my side.

Katie Fellows (9)

My Best Buddy

F antastic to play with
R unning and jumping with joy
I really, really like him
E ven though he can be annoying
N ot once has he let me down
D aring things he likes to do
S ure, Lewis is my best friend!

Ben Mason (9)

My Sister, Summer

My sister, Summer, she's so sweet,
I love her so much, but she's got stinky feet!

We were in Costas having a drink,
While she was on the bottle having a drink.

She's so cheeky, I love her so much,
She's noisy and playful and speaks double-Dutch!

Megan Conder (10)

Grandma

My grandma's my favourite person, her hugs and kisses are great,
I know she is my grandma and she's also my best mate.

She always smiles and makes me laugh and sometimes acts the fool,
And if I'm ever sad or scared she gives me cuddles too.

I bet you wish that you could have a grandma so unique,
But sorry you can't have her because she's mine to keep.

Courtney Hewitt (11)

My Favourite Person

M y gran is very special to me
Y ou can always trust her

G enuine, generous and great at cooking
R eally good to have in my family
A lways trying to make me happy
N ice and never naughty.

Jordan Russell (10)

Untitled

Dilon! Dilon! What a friend, always there to help me spend
Round the corner, up the street, on our bikes, more friends to meet
The park's the place we spend our time, playing on the grass in the sun shine
Battered swings, graffitied slide, rickety stairs but . . . who cares?
As my friends and I play, my mobile rings, it's Mum to say,
'Hurry home now, your tea is ready, we've decided to eat little Freddy!'

Ryan Hughes (11)

My Granny

G ranny, I love you
R eliable when I need her
A lways laughing
N ever cross at me
N ever forgets a hug
Y ou are the best granny to me.

Sarah Hagan (8)

Untitled

A friend is like a flower, a rose to be exact
Or maybe a brand new gate that never comes unlatched
A friend is like an owl, both beautiful and wise
Or perhaps a friend is like a ghost whose spirit never dies
A friend is like a heart, strong until the end
Where would we be in the world, if we didn't have a friend!

Stacy Senyonga (9)

My Little Dog

A silver, curly coat and a small, waggy tail,
She loves to go for walks, especially the woodland trails,
Soft, little paws and big, floppy ears,
Big puppy eyes that never shed tears,
She's got a little black nose and she sleeps like a log,
Her name is Poppy and she's my dog!

Jess Smith (11)

Ewan

E wan is my best mate
W e like playing on our bikes
A nd playing football
I n and out of school.

T ogether
H e
O ften
M akes me
P leasantly
S mile
O ur friendship will, I hope
N ever end.

Mitchel Bullion (10)
Dalreoch Primary School, Dumbarton

153

My Mum Is The Best

You are very smart
Also have a lovely heart

Nobody is to blame
That you are not the same

You like to trim my hair
No matter if I want it there

You are sometimes sneezy
But hardly breezy

You are a delight
And give Dougie a fright

You teach us to do
Very many things too!

You make me smile
Not just for a while

You make me laugh
Because you're daft!

Iona Taylor (10)
Dalreoch Primary School, Dumbarton

My Best Friend

K ian is my best friend
I 'll be his mate till the end.
A nd when I see him, he is very cool, I
N ever see him at school.

S oon I'll see him once again, unless
T he boy visits Big Ben.
R unning with a football one day
A s soon as I tackle him, he has a penalty.
I 'm in goal, he's outfield, the ball
N earing my face, as I kneel . . .

Kyle Furphy (10)
Dalreoch Primary School, Dumbarton

My Best Friend Eddy

My best friend is Eddy
He is small and steady
Never in a hurry
But still very funny
He's like a brother
That's why he's my friend Eddy.

He's weird but funny
Still like a bunny
He loves money
He loves honey – very runny
That's why he is my friend Eddy.

He loves to watch Mandy
And loves sweet and sour candy
He has the smallest handies
And still calls his pants panties
But he is still my best friends Eddy!

Liam Harris (10)
Dalreoch Primary School, Dumbarton

My Wonderful Mum

Oh my sweet, loving mum,
How you are such fun.
Oh how you make me laugh,
You are the best mum a girl could ever have.

You always make me smile,
Every once in a while.
You are the best mum ever,
You will be mine forever.

You always make me feel better,
By giving me a really warm sweater.
Oh Mum you are so clever,
The most wonderful mum ever!

Victoria Auld (10)
Dalreoch Primary School, Dumbarton

My Friend

I have friends
The special one
Is Dillon Young.

My friend
He says it's fun
Playing with a bun.

My special friend
He wrestles with his thumb
He thinks it is fun.

My friend
I think he's cool
He likes a swim in the pool.

My special friend
Is sometimes violent
As well as silent.

Bailey Hoyland (9)
Dalreoch Primary School, Dumbarton

My Amazing Mum

M y mum is the best in each and every way
Y *ay!*

A mazing mum, that's her name
M y mum rocks
A nd
Z *zzzzzzz*, will stay
I n bed all day
N ever will she make me sad
G rumble at me and make me mad

M y mum will always be the same
U nder the roof we're a family
M y mum's the best!

Christie Grierson (10)
Dalreoch Primary School, Dumbarton

Laura Ann

Laura Ann you are silly
You're just like Billy!

You spoil me
No matter what!

You will shout at me
But I know you won't mean it!

I always annoy Charley
And you will say, 'Stop it!'

When I come along
I will always help you

I take Charley out
So you can tidy up!

You drop the broom
And we dream of the moon!

Kiera Aitken (10)
Dalreoch Primary School, Dumbarton

Mum

My mum loves Home and Away,
She watches it every day,
She turns up the sound,
And it blows her away.

She does the washing, the cleaning,
Not to mention the feeding,
She cleans my room,
With her witch's broom!

My mum is very clever,
She will be mine forever,
She is very funny,
That's why I call her 'Mummy'.'

Dillon Young (9)
Dalreoch Primary School, Dumbarton

My Best Friend

Dean is tall and funny
Never small, always sunny
Never feeling down
Nor wears a frown
Dean is up
But never down
He has a pup
Small and brown
But that pup
Always has a frown
Give him food
And he will smile
The day is done
And so am I.

Benji Kelly (10)
Dalreoch Primary School, Dumbarton

My Big Brother

My big brother is the best
When I am with him I forget the rest.
My big brother is so smart
And he has such a big heart.
When we play
Every day
He is the best.
But he makes me treat him like a guest.
Watching him play the Xbox
He really rocks.
He is the best big brother
Just the same as my mother.
He is the best
When I'm with him I forget the rest!

Reece Smylie (9)
Dalreoch Primary School, Dumbarton

Marni

M arni is funny
A s her mummy
R eally funny
N ever nasty
I f she cries

M akes her happy
C uddly baby
I nside the house, she's hyper
N ever moody
T eatime is when she watches programmes
O n TV – she laughs
S leepy baby, sleeps all night
H appy as always.

Kayleigh McIntosh (9)
Dalreoch Primary School, Dumbarton

Laura

L aura and I laugh and play all night long
A nd it takes a long time to get Laura ready
U sually she hates tidying her room
R anging rudeness, very smelly
A nger around me.

M akes very good pancakes, and her
C akes are very nice
I n the house there is a mouse that Laura hates
N ext mouse tried to escape but Laura is scared
T ea time she watches TV like an insane alien
'Y ummy pancakes,' says Mummy
R ed rockets going into outer space
E xciting day ended at that moment. Fell asleep.

Caitlin King (10)
Dalreoch Primary School, Dumbarton

My Dad

My dad is really silly
He is just like Billy.
He is the best
But why does he wear a vest
In a test?

You are the best
You help me
With the rest of my test
You are the best

Of the family, Michael,
You are the best!

Nicole Davidson (11)
Dalreoch Primary School, Dumbarton

Niamh

N iamh Wright is my favourite person
I like her brown eyes
A s well as her blonde hair
M y favourite thing about her is friendship
H er friendship is always true.

W hen she laughs it tickles my tummy
R unning is her favourite thing
I love to play with her
G oes everywhere with her friends
H er sense of humour is hilarious
T he thing that she likes is friends!

Katie MacDonald (8)
Dalreoch Primary School, Dumbarton

Mum

Warm, gentle, generous and kind
She's the one I love deep inside
Always there when I need her
Mum, mum, lovely mum
Every night I get a cuddle and a kiss
Sweet as a rose
Day by day
I say I love her
Nothing can come between us
Mum, mum, mum
She is number one!

Jordan Rogerson (11)
Dalreoch Primary School, Dumbarton

A Friend And Fellow Classmate

My favourite person is Megan Smith
I used to believe friendship was a myth
If I fell over she would help me up
Made me laugh so hard I knocked over a cup
She is smart, funny and strong
We will be friends for very long
Megan is a friend and fellow classmate
Being her friend is really great
I stay at her house, she stays at mine
Talk to her in the line at school
She's my friend, she's super cool!

Caitlin McCulloch (11)
Dalreoch Primary School, Dumbarton

Taylor Opfer

T he sweet little devil,
A little candy drop,
Y oung and
O pen-minded,
R eally kind to me, and

O thers,
P laying all day without any bothers,
F it as a fiddle, Taylor Opfer,
E ver so playful and
R ough!

Alan Opfer (11)
Dalreoch Primary School, Dumbarton

My Fantastic Mum

My mum is good
She's never in a mood
My mum is silly
Like a boy called Billy
She has a bunny
Who is funny
My mum has a head
Which is never dead
She dances with Molly
We should have called her Polly!

Dylan Bolton (11)
Dalreoch Primary School, Dumbarton

Monica

Monica, Monica I think you're sweet and kind
Sometimes you are funny and emotional too.

You sometimes get serious like Julie or Aunty Fran
You like to play some stupid games
I think that's really fun
Just like when we were at your house
And had that fantastic water fight!

I think you are the best in the world
And that's coming from my heart.

Rachel Heaney (10)
Dalreoch Primary School, Dumbarton

My Best Friend

L ewis Robb is my best friend
E very time I'm bored we always play
W e always go to the field behind the park
 I enjoy playing with him
S uper fast runner

R ollerblades
R ock bands are his favourite
B ad at climbing
B ye-bye.

Liam Bell (10)
Dalreoch Primary School, Dumbarton

A Special Mum

My mum is special
She cares about me
She helps me
She loves me
She surprises me
She feeds me
She needs me
That is why
My mum is special to me.

Carly McCallum (9)
Dalreoch Primary School, Dumbarton

Ewan

Ewan is silly
He looks like Billy
He is that silly!
He is funny
He is Bugs Bunny
He hates honey!
He was climbing a tree
He was stung by a bee
When he fell and broke his knee!

Billy Weir (10)
Dalreoch Primary School, Dumbarton

Sam

S am is a very good friend to me
A lways there to play with when I am sad
M e and Sam are beasts together, we scare people and spy
                               on people as well.

Matthew McGroggan (8)
Dalreoch Primary School, Dumbarton

Brother

I love my brother so much
We fight but not all the time.
We have pillow fights that are so much fun
But at lunch he broke my thumb.

He has pink hair and looks very cool
But sometimes he can act like a fool.
When I was young he gave me hugs and kisses
But now he goes out on dates with his missus!

Julie Monaghan (10)
Dalreoch Primary School, Dumbarton

Catherine The Smarty Pants

Smart as a star shining bright,
Always right,
In the night,
A vampire that's what she's like,
My sister on her bike,
Speeding past,
As fast as light,
And, she always gets maths right.

Andrew Scarlett (11)
Dalreoch Primary School, Dumbarton

My Best Friend

Cassidy, Cassidy, you are my best friend
I think you're hilarious and funny too
When I need you you're always there to stand up for me
You're so special
Even though we fight
You're still my best friend ever.

Danielle Brown (9)
Dalreoch Primary School, Dumbarton

My Mum

Mum is her name, I use it every day.
She makes me laugh and giggle.
My mum is the best mum in the whole world.
Mum is my best friend.
Full of love and laughter in every way.
She is special in every way.
She is the one who brightens up my day.
And that's why I love her.

Eilidh Robertson (10)
Dalreoch Primary School, Dumbarton

My Mum

My mum is very funny
My mum always helps me
My mum hops about like a bunny
My mum jumps about like a flea
I know my mum loves me
She will shout at me but I know
She doesn't mean it
Because she loves me!

Erin Joyce (10)
Dalreoch Primary School, Dumbarton

Reece

R eece and I are always having fun
E very time he comes to my house we are doing experiments
on a fake mouse
E very day we play now and play fun games
C oming up to my house we are always having a laugh
E ntering my loft space, jumping up and down, it's a lot
of fun playing with Reece.

Jack Stopford (9)
Dalreoch Primary School, Dumbarton

Dad

Dad's got a smile that lights up.
He's never down in the dumps.
Dad's got a shirt that's always tucked in.
He's always having good fun.
Dad always plays his Xbox 360.
He likes a chocolate Crunchie.
Dad likes the colour green.
He doesn't like to be mean.

Tyra Ross (11)
Dalreoch Primary School, Dumbarton

My Proud Brother

I am proud of my brother.
He is in the army fighting for our country.
On hills, on water, he will never give up.
He will fight with everything he has.

I'm sure he's proud too.
I will never forget him.
I'm sure he's fine but now it's his time to shine.

Dean Allardice (10)
Dalreoch Primary School, Dumbarton

World's Best Nan

Gran has soft, brown, curly hair,
She has a smooth oval face.
Rosy cheeks and pretty lipstick too!
Her eyes are as big as disco balls.

My nan is a kind, generous person, helpful too!
She does the most fabulous cooking.
The house is always spick and span,
Sister reunions with tea and cakes too.

She lives in quite a lively estate,
On the outskirts of a small village.
Only a bus ride from town.
She's pleased when we come down!

My nan loves me and I love my nan.

Sophie Higgins (11)
Somerton Primary School, Newport

My Incredible Nan

My nan's scarf is black, long and sparkly,
She has grey, curly hair,
Her eyes are as big as pennies,
Her face is oval, smooth and brown.

Her dress is black and glossy gold,
She wears grey shiny sandals,
She drinks milky tea,
And loves to eat pizza too!

She loves to work all the time,
She enjoys spending time in the garden,
She is a very proud lady,
And I love my nan.

Lucman Abedin (9)
Somerton Primary School, Newport

168

My Beautiful Nan

Gran has long, white, curly hair
She has an oval, wrinkly face
Her eyes are like two buttons
Her skin is brown, like a chocolate cake.

She wears soft saris with nice black sandals
And with plenty of bangles
She sometimes wears glasses for reading in bed
Or watching her favourite TV channel!

She lives in the city of London
She likes to spend time in her garden
There's a lot of buildings around her
And plenty of bushes too.

Fahima Ahmed (9)
Somerton Primary School, Newport

Number One Gran

Gran has short, brown, silky hair
Her eyes are big, brown and glossy too
She wears brown trousers and tops and cardigans too
And lovely brown and gold shoes.

She loves planting and growing flowers
She loves going out in the fresh breeze
She has a very good job
And looks out for other people.

My gran has a good life
Her house is very nice
She bakes yummy cookies for me
She is the best soft-hearted nan!

Abbey Farmer (10)
Somerton Primary School, Newport

My Super Gran

My gran has eyes as big as a balloon
My gran has red rosy cheeks
My gran has long, beautiful hair
My gran has tanned skin.

My gran wears short, baggy jeans
My gran wears colourful tops
My gran watches lots of TV
My gran does lots of shopping

My gran likes to walk to different places
My gran like to cook early in the morning
My gran loves real rubies
My gran's house is as big as a castle.

Liam Gale (11)
Somerton Primary School, Newport

My Best Nan

My gran has soft, short, curly hair
Her eyes are as small as dewdrops
She wears dresses the colours of rainbows
Red, orange, green, purple and yellow.

She has a sister called Ruby
She enjoys cooking with her sister too
Her favourite drink is milky tea
Or a can of Diet Coke!

She always enjoys reading
My gran is so loving and caring
She never stops working
She likes to relax, once in a while!

Nicole McCarthy (9)
Somerton Primary School, Newport

My Amazing Grandmother

Gran has short, reddish brown hair
Her eyes are as small as pearls
She has a thin oval face, her skin is quite brown
She is allergic to the sun, a vast amount.

She wears small cardigans – so small they fit me!
She wears plain tops that have petite patterns
She wears crop trousers as small as can be
She wears shoes as flat as a stingray.

She eats a lot of organic foods
She likes tea and coffee, she reads a lot every day
She gives me and my mum clothes
She spends a lot of time cleaning.

Ffion Williams (9)
Somerton Primary School, Newport

My Super Nanny

Gran has long, blonde, straight hair
Her eyes are as blazing as the sun
Her dress is as bright as flowers
Gran has shoes as soft as roses.

My nanny's favourite food is faggots
She likes to drink tea or wine!
She loves to clean her house
My nanny loves having guests to visit.

She likes to boogie to Michael Jackson
In her big new house
She always has a duster to hand
To make it spick and span!

Madeline Thomson (9)
Somerton Primary School, Newport

My Loving Nan

Gran has long, straight, grey hair
Her eyes are as big as the ocean
Her face is oval and bright as the sun

Gran wears baggy jeans and pretty tops
She does the shopping at Tesco
She likes to eat fish and chips

Gran likes to watch the musicals
And play bingo
She also likes to cook.

I love my nan.

Aimee Worrell (10)
Somerton Primary School, Newport

My Great Nan

Gran looks like a beautiful summer rose,
Her lips are as red as a strawberry,
Her eyes are like sparkling diamonds,
She has grey, curly hair.

Her cheeks are like oranges,
Her nails are painted like bright rubies,
Her nose is soft and beautiful,
Her face is like the sun.

My nan is a kind, helpful person,
She is beautiful in all kinds of ways.

Lewis Fry (10)
Somerton Primary School, Newport

Young Writers Information

We hope you have enjoyed reading this
book - and that you will continue to enjoy it
in the coming years.

If you like reading and writing poetry drop us
a line, or give us a call, and we'll send you a
free information pack.

Alternatively if you would like to order further
copies of this book or any of our other titles, then
please give us a call or log onto our website at
www.youngwriters.co.uk

Young Writers Information
Remus House
Coltsfoot Drive
Peterborough
PE2 9JX
(01733) 890066